52 SAINTS TO PRAY WITH

Jean Marie Hiesberger

PAULIST PRESS
New York/Mahwah, NJ

Cover Art: *Our Lady, Queen of the Missions* by Aleksandra Kasuba (b. 1923) and manufactured by Venetian Art Mosaics Studios of New York City. © Basilica of the National Shrine of the Immaculate Conception, Washington, DC. Used with permission. All rights reserved.

Cover design by Sharyn Banks
Book design by Lynn Else

Library of Congress Cataloging-in-Publication Data

Hiesberger, Jean Marie.
    52 saints to pray with / Jean Marie Hiesberger.
        p. cm.
    title: Fifty two saints to pray with
    ISBN 978-0-8091-4648-2 (alk. paper)
    1. Christian saints—Biography. 2. Christian life—Catholic
authors. I. Title. II. Title: Fifty two saints to pray with.
    BX4655.3.H54 2010
    282.092′2—dc22
    [B]

                                                    2009047947

Published by Paulist Press
997 Macarthur Boulevard
Mahwah, New Jersey 07430

www.paulistpress.com

Printed and bound in the
United States of America

TABLE OF CONTENTS

PREFACE

This is a book for people who are busy, perhaps too busy to read a volume about the lives of the saints, but who want to try to live as Christ wants them to live and could use a little encouragement and help in how to do that. Here we find examples of ordinary and extraordinary people who can provide exactly that kind of support.

Each page in this little volume follows the same three-part pattern:

1. First, there is a brief summary of the person's life.
2. This is followed by a paragraph or two that looks at the person's life from the perspective of the essence of what makes him or her someone of note for us.
3. Finally, there are concrete suggestions for how we can follow these examples in our lives today. This is just a starting point. You will undoubtedly find other insights and ideas to take from these extraordinary/ordinary people to help you along your own life path.

My hope is that this glimpse into the lives of admirable Christians will be a helpful reminder that holiness is found in the ordinary events and people along the path each of us walks every day. The use of models or heroes/heroines demonstrates the virtues needed to live a Christian life but reminds us that we do not have to be an extraordinary person to live a holy or saintly life.

Holiness comes not only in all shapes and sizes but also in as many different ways of living as there are people and personalities. The particular virtues lived and individual roads chosen will reflect how God has blessed each person with specific talents and unique opportunities to live out their lives.

ALPHONSUS LIGUORI
(1696–1787)

Who He Was

Alphonsus Liguori was a brilliant young lawyer in Naples, Italy, but not for long. He soon gave up his practice of law and joined a group of mission preachers. After he was ordained a priest, he organized a group of religious sisters and later a group of priests to go from place to place to preach the Gospel. Alphonsus desired very good preaching so that all the people could understand the message of the Gospel. He was very critical of priests who celebrated the mass very quickly, or those who preached in a way that made the gospel message hard to understand or did not apply it to life.

Alphonsus was a very popular preacher as well as a moral theologian who had a doctoral degree in Canon Law. He believed moral theology was more about the practical and concrete problems of people and that it should be applied with simplicity and kindness rather than a rigid law. His most important work, *Moral Theology*, was reprinted nine times during his life. It was one of his thirty-six published works.

Pope Pius XII named him the patron saint of moral theologians in 1950.

Alphonsus' later life was filled with great hardship and suffering. He signed a document, apparently due to misunderstanding and to his very bad eyesight, which split the Redemptorist community into separate groups. To his great sorrow, the two parts were not reunited until after his death in 1787. However, Pope Pius VI, the same person who had spoken against his signing of the document that split his community, later did all he could to have him named a saint. The Redemptorists, the community that Alphonsus founded, are still held in high regard to this day for their fine preaching.

His Life Speaks to Me

Alphonsus Liguori's life certainly had its highs and lows. He experienced great success as a lawyer and was greatly popular as a preacher. His writings were not only numerous, but he had the great satisfaction of knowing how helpful they were to many, many people. We can only imagine how crushed he felt when he discovered the document he signed actually divided his community. In his later years, he experienced great physical suffering from rheumatic fever that left him crippled for a time.

Following His Example

Life is uneven. Each of us experiences highs and lows in our life. While our lives may not be as serious and dramatic as Alphonsus, his example can inspire us to keep going when encountering an unexpected hardship in our path of life.

Being mindful to be attentive to the good things we experience and to be grateful for the blessings, he reminds us that life will not always be easy and pleasant, and we should not become resentful when people or events disappoint us. Every day of our life, we can follow the example of Alphonsus, who insisted that the message of Jesus Christ is one that is very practical, and we can continue to discover how we can live this message in our ordinary daily life.

✥

ANTHONY OF PADUA (1195–1231)

Who He Was

If people were asked who was one of the greatest preachers in the history of the Church, they would probably be surprised with the answer St. Anthony. He would be more likely to be mentioned as the saint to whom one prays when you have lost something. Like many people, Anthony's initial goal in life changed dramatically because of circumstances beyond his control. He desperately wanted to become a missionary so he joined the Franciscans and sailed to Morocco. However, that plan was never meant to be. Anthony became ill and needed to return to Portugal. However, his ship was blown off course and he ended up in Sicily rather than Portugal. From there he traveled north to Assisi where his religious superiors assigned him to a small hermitage where he lived quietly for some time.

Anthony was a gifted scripture scholar and remarkable preacher. These talents were discovered when he was asked to preach at an ordination ceremony on short notice. Many Franciscans, a bishop, and some Dominicans heard him. This resulted in his travel through Lombardy, where his preaching attracted thousands of people. As provincial leader of the Franciscans in the north, he went to Rome, where his preaching was described as a "jewel case of the Bible." Today you can read his "Sermons for Feast Days." Anthony's last sermons were principally directed against hatred for others.

True to the Franciscan spirit, Anthony worked on behalf of the poor. He helped those in debt by getting a law passed that allowed them to sell their possessions to pay their debts so they would not be imprisoned, as was the custom. His concern for the poor is remembered today in St. Anthony's Bread, a movement to help the starving, especially in the Third World. Today huge loaves of bread in the shape of a crown are baked in Sicily on June 13, his feast day.

His Life Speaks to Me

Anthony's many qualities of human goodness give many options for all people in all times to imitate wherever they live. He took his studies seriously and developed the talent and skills God placed in him—in his case, the gift of preaching. He became involved in the political process to get unfair laws changed and did what he could for those who were hungry for bread as well as those who were hungry to hear the Good News preached.

Following His Example

People who do not have enough to eat are inevitably without a voice in creating or changing unjust laws. Those who are well fed are called to help feed the hungry in two ways. The first way is through practical actions such as donations, volunteer efforts, and organizing food banks in our parishes. Secondly, like Anthony we are called to work in changing the system that keeps so many children and adults in our society without enough on the table. Working with grass-roots political groups and being conscientious about voting for just laws are simple ways each of us can imitate St. Anthony of Padua. We can also follow his example by speaking out against hatred directed at individuals and groups.

✦

BARTOLOMÉ DE LAS CASAS (1484–1566)

Who He Was

Bartolomé de Las Casas was a boy in Spain when he saw Christopher Columbus return to Seville after his first voyage to the New World. As a teenager, he made the long boat trip to Hispaniola. Later Bartolomé studied in Rome for the priesthood and served as chaplain in the Spanish conquest of Cuba. For this service, he was rewarded with an *encomienda*, a plantation with Indian indentured laborers. Las Casas witnessed the genocide of the Indians in Cuba. This experience horrified him and resulted in a dramatic conversion in which Bartolomé became a member of the Dominican religious community who was a strong and outspoken defender of the native people in the New World. He tried to stop the cruelties, including the slaughtering of the locals by the Spanish. He wrote letters and made visits to the court of Spain. However, the pope had approved subjugating the Indian people in the name of spreading the Gospel and making converts.

Some people claimed that these native peoples were a lesser race, but Bartolomé strongly defended their human rights and equality. His experience convinced him that social justice must be part of salvation in Jesus Christ. In an attempt to get him out of the way, Bartolomé was named bishop of Chiapas, Mexico. However, while there he was threatened with death when he refused absolution to any Spaniard who would not free his slaves. Finally, Bartolomé resigned as bishop and returned to Spain, where he died at the age of eighty-two.

His Life Speaks to Me

Fighting for a just cause against huge odds for your entire life, as Bartolomé did, is something very few human beings have undertaken. Nothing and no one would deter Bartolomé from what he believed in. Throughout his entire life as a young man until his death in his eighties, Bartolomé de Las Casas never stopped speaking against injustice and working to right the wrongs he had seen. This was not for himself, because he could have had a comfortable life; it was for those who had no voice and no power against the powerful. He never gave up or slowed down, even though the odds were insurmountable. Whether or not he helped the native peoples, he has given a gift to us by the example of his life. The Church proclaims Bartolomé a model for us to follow. Like him, each of us, in our own way, must work for social justice.

Following His Example

Where do we see injustice? Where do we see someone without a voice? We must pay attention to discover the answer. Wherever we see such things, we can remember Bartolomé de Las Casas and respond. Whether it is in the setting of a family, school, work, our city or town, the person who notices and speaks out about injustices is needed. As Bartolomé taught, our mission is both to take action and to be a voice for those who have the ability to make needed changes. Bartolomé worked to open the eyes and hearts of those in power, especially those who had a duty to care for people in need and who failed to do so. We, too, can take such actions. For us, it may take expression by writing a letter to the editor of a newspaper, making a phone call to a political representative, or joining a parish social action committee.

✠

BONAVENTURE
(1221–1274)

Who He Was

In 1265, Pope Clement IV nominated the Franciscan scholar, Bonaventure, to be archbishop of York. Bonaventure declined. Less than ten years later, it happened again; this time, Bonaventure was named cardinal-bishop of Albano. Because it was the thirteenth century, a time in which postal services or e-mail communication did not exist, the Pope sent his messengers to inform Bonaventure. When they arrived at his friary near Florence, Italy, the emissaries found Bonaventure washing the dishes. He told them that they needed to wait until he finished his task to meet with him. It is not surprising that this man, who had been the leader of the Franciscan Order since he was thirty-six, is the patron saint of workers.

Bonaventure is considered one of the great theologians in the history of the Church. He was the master of the Franciscan school in Paris and a friend of St. Thomas Aquinas. As a theologian, Bonaventure understood that the purpose of studying theology and even more so, the purpose of all human learning, was to love. He balanced both the intellect and rational side with the affect or emotions in the study of God.

Bonaventure is considered as the second founder of the Franciscan Order. During his time as the community's leader, the Franciscans split into two parts. One group took the life of poverty literally—including not owning possessions or property as well as also not being involved in learning or pastoral ministry. Others saw the need to have property such as schools and universities for educating the young while continuing to live simply and humbly themselves. They also wanted the Franciscans to be involved in pastoral ministry, preaching, and spiritual direction. Today there are many Franciscan schools and universities in which their members are leaders in various and different ministries.

His Life Speaks to Me

Bonaventure seemed destined for leadership positions: master of the Paris School, leader of his religious order, adviser to the pope at the Second Council of Lyons, reconciler between the churches of the East and West as well as within the Franciscan Order. Yet this man with great intellectual gifts and leadership skills remained humble. Taking turns at dishwashing is a symbol of the perspective of how he viewed himself personally. Bonaventure took a position of balance, whether in his theology of mind and affect or balancing the Franciscan spirit of simplicity and poverty while using their talents at the service of the Church through institutions.

Following His Example

Humility can be a misunderstood virtue. Like Bonaventure, we can fully use our talents and skills without expecting to be honored or letting our success go to our head. Both our mind and our emotions are needed in our faith so that it is not just "from the neck up." What we know and believe are to be integrated into who we are, how we treat others, and how we live our typical days. Using both our heart and our head in faith and in life makes us more like Bonaventure and more like Christ.

⟨⊕⟩

CARLOS RODRÍGUEZ SANTIAGO (1918–1963)

Who He Was

Suffering was no stranger to Carlos Rodríguez Santiago. As a six-year-old boy in Puerto Rico, both his family's home and store were burned to the ground. A serious illness interrupted his high school years. Eventually he finished high school and wanted to attend the university. After another delay, Carlos' health prevented him from going beyond the first year of studies at the University of Puerto Rico. He was both brilliant and in poor health. Severe chronic ulcerative colitis caused him suffering and inconvenience throughout his whole life. He died of rectal cancer in 1963 at the age of forty-four.

A quiet, shy man and a devout person from early in his life, Carlos taught himself to play the piano and became an avid reader who enjoyed all kinds of literature. He learned to translate documents from English to Spanish and worked as an office clerk. Carlos' special interest was the Sacred Liturgy and he began translating articles on this important topic. He started a student group at the university whose members studied and promoted the liturgy, especially the active participation of the laity and the use of the vernacular language in liturgy rather than Latin. Known for his great smile and personal joy, he suffered through a period during his life when he doubted God's presence. Eventually, he rediscovered the Word of God and experienced a return of peace and joy.

His Life Speaks to Me

Carlos had a brief and unusual life. While it may seem quite different from ours, we share with him the fact that life brings about unexpected challenges. Our challenge may not be chronic, serious illness like his or a dream disappointed because of not completing our education. However, in the course of every life there are disappointments, obstacles, and challenges of various kinds. Rather than saying, "Why me?" like Carlos we can say, "Why not me?" We may not get to choose the cross we bear but we do have a choice in how we bear it. Like Carlos, we can take comfort, inspiration, and hope from the liturgy, especially the Eucharist. Similar to him, we may even have a "dark night of the soul" when we doubt and wonder where God is, but if we stay on course with our faith and don't become bitter or cynical, we will pass through that challenging time just as Carlos did.

Following His Example

Carlos illustrates the bumper sticker message, "When life gives you lemons, make lemonade." The difficulties we experience can discourage us and drag us into self-pity if we allow them to. They can also raise us up to new directions and discoveries if we use our faith and our talents to move forward. Like Carlos, we have the great gifts of the Eucharist and the other sacraments to sustain us during difficult times and to keep us strong and close to Christ during other times. The more we learn about the sacraments and experience them, the more their richness will carry over into our daily life, no matter what we face.

✠

CATHERINE DOHERTY (1896–1985)

Who She Was

Catherine Doherty was a woman who experienced enough in a single lifetime to cover the lives of several people. She lived in several countries as well as living through two World Wars, the Russian Revolution, and the Great Depression in the United States. She knew what it was to be a refugee, to face the challenges of single parenthood and a broken marriage. She experienced a life of both in extreme poverty and great wealth.

This Russian-born woman grew up in an aristocratic family, which enabled her to live well and travel extensively in her youth. During the Russian Revolution, many of her family members were killed and she and her family narrowly escaped. They fled first to England and then to Canada, where she lived in dramatic poverty as she struggled to support her sick husband and their child. Her experience convinced her that the Russian Bolshevik Revolution was a result of the failure of Christians to live what the Gospel teaches about caring for the poor and needy, about professing to believe but not acting against racial injustice, secularism, and economic injustices, as Christ wants us to. Catherine's mission in life became to live a radical Gospel life and to recognize God's image in every human being. Throughout her life, Catherine cried out against the hypocrisy of those who professed to follow Christ while failing to serve him in others.

Her Life Speaks to Me

Catherine's faith was so strong and compelling that she tried to live the gospel message of social justice by living simply and reaching out to the poor in very real and concrete ways. However, this was not enough for her and she decided to gather other committed Catholics to share in this mission together, to develop their prayer life and spirituality, and to support each other in caring for the poor.

To achieve this end, she established the Friendship House movement in Canada and the United States. In 1955, she founded Madonna House. Today Madonna House has approximately two hundred members, including clergy and laypeople who come from many backgrounds and share a life of prayer and service to the poor.

Following Her Example

Catherine's life speaks to all who call themselves a Christian, not because everyone devotes their lives to social justice as she did but because her life points out the importance of what Christ gave as the criteria for being a Christian: feeding the hungry, visiting the imprisoned, caring for those in need, and fighting all the social justice issues that cry out for our help. Knowing that Catherine lived a radical lifestyle as her way of following Christ can give us motivation and courage to do all we can in our own way.

❧

CATHERINE OF SIENA (1347–1380)

Who She Was

Catherine of Siena had more than two dozen siblings. However, this was just the first unusual thing about her short life of thirty-three years. One of the youngest in her family, she was expected to marry into a wealthy Italian family. She

tations of them. Clare had many suitors, but she took a dramatic action that Lent when she heard Francis preach. She literally ran away from home one night to the Franciscan Chapel of St. Mary of the Angels. There she sheared her long hair and traded her elegant clothes for a simple dress. Her family, furious at her decision, tracked her down and tried to coerce her back home. However, she had made a final decision to join Francis and live in the gospel manner as he and his followers did. Clare and Francis remained close friends for many years. He trusted her wisdom and advice. Clare urged Francis to go out into the world to preach his message.

In her community of nuns, eventually called the Poor Clares, Clare served the sick, waited on the tables of those who came to be fed, and washed the feet of the nuns who went out to beg for food. Even when Pope Gregory IX tried to absolve her from her vow of poverty, she was steadfast, telling him, "I wish to be absolved from my sins but not from the obligation of following Christ this way." By the time of her death, there were Poor Clares in Italy, France, and Germany.

Her Life Speaks to Me

Clare was a person of prayer from an early age. She took her spiritual life seriously as a laywoman and nourished it throughout her entire lifetime, not stopping her formation after childhood but continuing to learn and pray. Clare had a strong sense of who she was and paid attention to what she believed was the right thing for her to do. We do not know that Clare was not afraid of the radical choices she made, but we do know that she persisted in them and that her persistence was coupled with prayer. Like so many leaders, she never set out to lead, but simply to follow what she perceived she was called to do with her life. Her personal qualities along with her commitment to prayer made Clare a leader both in her own community and among popes and bishops, who came for her counsel.

Following Her Example

Few of us choose to live the life of extreme poverty that Clare lived, yet her example can help us examine how we might live more simply and share some of what we have with those in greater need. Clare did not have the support of her family with her life's decision, but fortunately she had the courage to follow what she believed. We can support someone who needs encouragement to follow one's heart and personal decision, someone who just needs another person to believe in them. Like Clare, each of us needs to continue personal formation and spiritual development. This may be done through spiritual reading, small group sharing, classes, and prayer to continue to mature in your own faith.

✠

DAMIEN OF MOLOKAI
(1840–1899)

Who He Was

In the nineteenth century when Father Damien De Veuster lived, leprosy was a contagious and untreatable disease. During that time, the population of the Hawaiian Islands was dramatically reduced because of disease, including leprosy. People who had this disease were forcibly taken and sent off to live together on a remote island called Molokai. In fact, they were literally dumped in the nearby water and left to make their own way, living in caves or shacks with no outside help. An amazing young priest from Belgium asked to be assigned to go to Molokai to live and minister to the lepers there. It took several years, but Damian led the people there in building clean places to live and in working together to become a community.

Even though the physical effects of leprosy horribly deformed its victims, Damien treated each person with utter respect and never avoided physical contact, even knowing how contagious leprosy was. The inevitable happened. Damien literally became one of them when he himself contracted the dreaded disease. Although his courage and fame had spread well beyond the islands and his home in Belgium, he became exiled. Damien worked tirelessly to care for his diseased community members until he died of leprosy in 1899, long after this Belgian farm boy had said good-bye to his family and the life everyone expected him to live.

His Life Speaks to Me

Damien made a series of decisions in his life, each of which led him down an unknown path. He left his family and his home country to become a missionary priest. He lived through that separation not knowing how permanent it would become due to the next decision. He volunteered for the assignment to help the people of Molokai. Although it may seem to us that he would never return, it may have not been so clear to him. Once there, he gave himself entirely, working to serve and improve the lives of the suffering men, women, and children, as well as making this desolate place one where each person was respected. He kept his faith and his spirit of hope under these challenging conditions.

Following His Example

Leaving one's family and friends is never easy. However, Damien's example gives us courage when we feel alone and disconnected. As our world becomes smaller and smaller and we become more aware of different kinds of people, Damien's acceptance of every person and lack of prejudice toward those who are different can remind us to keep both our own minds and hearts open, free of judgment and prejudice. In addition, the wholehearted way Damien took on his difficult work can encourage us if we find ourselves in work that is trying or unfulfilling, in studies that are not easy and of great interest, or in any situation over which we have little control. Like Damien, we can do our best, knowing that dealing with life itself can reward us by making us stronger and better people.

✠

DOM HÉLDER CÂMARA (1909–1999)

Who He Was

Archbishop Câmara was the former archbishop of Olinda and Recife, the poorest and least developed region in Brazil. Frequently described as "one of the shapers of the Catholic Church in the second half of the twentieth century," he was one of the most influential figures of the progressive wing of the Second Vatican Council and an outspoken champion of the poor and oppressed. He worked to improve the lives of indigent people, not only in his native Brazil, but also throughout the world. Câmara's command of several languages, which he learned in the seminary, was a great help to him as a leader in the world at large. He was quite skilled at organizing and was one of the founders of CELAM (*Consejo Episcopal Latinoamericano*), the organization of Latin American bishops.

In Recife, he avoided wearing the archbishop's purple sash and refused to live in the archbishop's palace. Instead, he lived in a church hidden away in a poor area, taking his meals with the taxi drivers at their stall across the road. These unusual actions were sincere and not for external show. Câmara gave Church land away for a settlement for the poor and started a credit union for them. He had seminarians come out of their hidden seminaries and live in small communities in parishes. He believed in educating the laity and set up a theological institute for laypeople and priests, though these last two actions were later undone by his successors. Always concerned for the poor, he criticized the 1964 military coup that took over Brazil. The government leaders sent agents to murder him and while they brutally killed his young priest assistant, they could not bring themselves to kill Câmara. They later confessed and asked his forgiveness. Archbishop Câmara died in 1999 at the age of 90.

One of his most famous statements is "When I give food to the poor, they call me a saint. When I ask why the poor have no food, they call me a communist."

His Life Speaks to Me

Dom Hélder Câmara was a person who had the courage of his convictions. Though it cost him dearly, he stood up to leaders both in the Church and the government in his quest to follow the gospel mandate to care for the poor and hungry. Reading about Archbishop Câmara can inspire us to examine our own convictions and how well we put them into action. Anyone who looks at Câmara's life—how he lived and what he did—can see exactly what his personal convictions were.

Following His Example

The popular saying from the past among teachers applies to all of us, "What you *are*, what you *do*, shouts so loudly that I cannot hear what you say." It can be intimidating to look at our life this way, but it can also give us motivation, energy, and courage. If we spend time reminding ourselves of our convictions about living a good life, we may be surprised. Oftentimes we are doing more than we thought. It can also help us see how much more we could do to put our actions in line with our convictions, just as Dom Hélder Câmara did.

✦

DON BOSCO (1815–1888)

Who He Was

All over the world today, thousands of children who are poor, abandoned, and at risk are given help and a chance in life primarily due to John Bosco. His own father died in 1817 when John was just a toddler, and his family experienced the desperate poverty prevalent then in Turin, Italy. During his youth, John had many jobs as a youngster to pay for his own education. He decided at a young age that he needed to go to school because he wanted to be a priest. The daily routine that became necessary to reach this goal was school, work as a waiter or other job, and study late into the night.

During that time in northern Italy, there was a great deal of chaos, poverty, and even revolution. As a result, hundreds of young people lived alone on the streets and under bridges in hopelessness. Now a priest, John, or "Don" (Italian for Father) Bosco, was horrified at the terrible lives of these children and teenagers. He saw not only their needs but also their potential. So, he began to gather them, giving them food, teaching them to read and write, and starting trade schools so they could develop skills.

Over time others joined in his efforts and those who stayed eventually became the Salesian Society, named after St. Francis de Sales, their patron. The mission was clear: offer friendship to the poor and abandoned youngsters. Don Bosco developed a pastoral approach for the Salesians in their ministry to the young: reason, religion, and kindness. His vision and work continues today.

His Life Speaks to Me

Don Bosco would say to the teens that no one loved: "It is enough to know that you are young and abandoned, for me to love you very much." His passion was to give to young people in need a chance at a full life. His mission crosses time and place. Unfortunately, the problems Don Bosco saw and responded to seem to be with us always. However, his focus is a model for us to open our eyes to the needs of others and do something, helping in whatever way we can, no matter how limited. He knew the value of life, all life, regardless of circumstances. He honored it and brought it to full potential in the children he served.

Following His Example

"Reason, religion and kindness" the motto of Don Bosco for teaching the youth in his care, is a good motto for each of us to live by. To continue to learn, especially about our faith, what it means, what it demands of us, what it gives to us, will help us live as an example of the kindness that Jesus brought to those around him. There are many youth in our time and our country who are as desperate as those Don Bosco found under the bridges in Turin in the 1800s. Through our church, Catholic Charities, and civic organizations, we can do our part to help make a difference to them.

✠

DOROTHY DAY (1897–1980)

Who She Was

Dorothy Day was standing in the Catholic Worker House dining room patiently listening to an incoherent man talking incessantly. A visitor tried to interrupt and she signaled for him to wait. When the conversation ended, she turned to the visitor and asked, "Now, which one of us are you waiting to speak to?" This was the kind of total respect Dorothy had for those who came for food or shelter. As a child on Chicago's South Side, she had known extreme poverty. A difficult path brought her to the point of full-time service to the poor. In 1917, she picketed the White House, protesting the brutal treatment of women suffragists in jail and served thirty days in a workhouse. In her younger years, she had a series of lovers, became pregnant, and had an illegal abortion.

The major turning point in her life was when she became pregnant again, decided to have the child, and subsequently left the child's father when he refused to let her have the child baptized. Dorothy had been studying the faith and joined the Church. Motherhood brought her to see the aimlessness of her life and, on December 8, at the Shrine of the Immaculate Conception, she prayed in tears to know how she should use her talents to help the poor.

Upon her return to New York, Peter Maurin encouraged Dorothy to use her journalistic skill to start the *Catholic Worker* newspaper, which she did. The Catholic Worker House she started in the New York slums is replicated in many places today to house and feed the homeless and hungry. "What we would like to do is change the world—make it a little simpler for people to feed, clothe, and shelter themselves as God intended them to do," she said. Dorothy died in 1980. After a lifetime of voluntary poverty, she left no money for her funeral. The Archdiocese of New York paid for it.

Her Life Speaks to Me

Dorothy used her remarkable intellect to teach through her publication. She used her basic humanness to connect with people who had little or nothing. Dorothy used the two-step method of combating poverty. On the one hand, she literally fed the poor and sheltered the homeless. On the other hand, she worked through her writing and her speeches to change the structures that made Catholic Worker Houses necessary. She asked, "Why was so much done in remedying the evil of poverty instead of avoiding it in the first place? Why don't people try to change the social order, not just to minister to the slaves, but to do away with slavery?"

Following Her Example

If everyone who believes in Jesus Christ used Dorothy Day's two-step method, perhaps her dream, as well as Christ's, would become a reality. Imagine, the impact it would have if every Christian would commit to help feed the hungry and shelter the homeless. If each of us used our voice even a little bit to speak up and to improve the obstacles that keep so many from being self-sufficient, it could make a difference.

✠

DOROTHY STANG (1931–2005)

Who She Was

Dorothy grew up helping her father work in his organic garden in Ohio. She was the fourth of five children in a Catholic family and learned from her father the importance of service, especially service to the poor. This peaceful, small town upbringing was a far cry from the end of her life, which found her on a dusty road in Brazil shot point blank by murderers precisely because she cared for and served the poor farmers there.

Dorothy had joined the Sisters of Notre Dame de Namur. For thirty years, she worked in Brazil even to the point of becoming a citizen there. Why was she murdered? The specific reason was that she was hated by the landowners and loggers who wanted the land of the small farms in order to cut down and sell the trees and reap the riches of minerals there. On repeated occasions, the small farmers were forced at gunpoint to abandon their farms and move deeper into the forest. Dorothy moved with them only to be forced off the next farms. She also fought for land reform so that the laws and government would protect the rural poor families from this repeated terrorism.

The larger reason Dorothy's life ended this way was that she believed deeply in the cause for which she gave her life. She saw a serious injustice being done and refused to walk away, even when she received death threats from the hired vigilantes.

Her Life Speaks to Me

This woman who loved ice cream and was said to make great pancakes had the courage of her convictions. She was fortunate to be a person who was clear about what those convictions were. She knew that her focus was service to the poor. Even when confronted by her killers she opened her Bible and read, "Blessed are the peacemakers....Blessed are the poor in spirit." The first step in even coming close to imitating someone like Dorothy Stang is to clarify our values and identify the principles that we want to guide our lives, no matter what.

Following Her Example

Like Dorothy, some people are quite aware of what their life-guiding values are. Others are not. When we take the time, do the work to articulate for ourselves what are our primary values, we give ourselves a much greater chance to follow them daily. Being consciously aware of them, these values can give us the energy and the strength to put them into practice. Ask yourself: What do I believe in? What am I willing to speak out for, to stand up for, or perhaps to dedicate my life to? What kind of service can I offer to others? At the end of your life, you will know exactly how to answer the question: "What did I try to do with my life?"

✣

EDITH STEIN (1891–1942)

Who She Was

Imagine a Jewish woman who was a university scholar, became a Catholic, entered the Carmelites, and had her life ended in a Nazi concentration camp. This was the life of Edith Stein, and it almost seems to read like a book of fiction or a movie script. She grew up in a large Jewish family in Breslau, Poland. By the time she was a teen, however, she considered herself an atheist. Edith was a brilliant student and studied philosophy as one of the first women even allowed to study in the University in Germany. It was when she read the autobiography of St. Teresa of Avila that she realized she wanted to be a Catholic. Not only that, Edith wanted to join the Carmelites of St. Teresa, which she did some years later.

It pained her Jewish family that she, and later her sister, would become Catholics and enter the convent during the very time of Nazi persecution of Jews. However, after the Catholic bishops in Holland strongly criticized the Nazis, the Nazis rounded up Jewish converts to Christianity and executed them. This included Edith, who was then fifty years old, as well as her sister. Before becoming a nun at the age of forty-two, Edith was a leading voice in the women's movement. Her writings on women have been very important for overcoming prejudices against women and recognizing them as equal and capable. Edith made a powerful case for women to be educated, believing strongly that "there is no profession which cannot be practiced by a woman."

She had a special interest in the notion of empathy, which enables us to understand another person clearly. This led her to encourage women to be involved in political life and leadership roles wherever they were. She believed that the experience of empathy was important in leadership, especially during "dark times," as she described them. On October 11, 1998, Edith Stein, also known by her religious name Sister Theresa Benedicta of the Cross, was declared a saint.

Her Life Speaks to Me

In many places in the world, the opportunity for receiving a good education is not open to women. Even in countries where it is an option, there are more barriers to women than men when it comes to higher education and professions. Edith broke such a barrier and then gave a helping hand to others to follow her lead. She also gives us a good example of overcoming prejudice. As an atheist, she allowed herself to be open to the opposite point of view. She talked with Christians to understand them and allowed herself to be changed dramatically. She worked hard to help others overcome their prejudices about women, breaking the barrier of prejudice at the university and spending years teaching and writing to help others overcome such prejudices.

Following Her Example

Like Edith, each of us can give a helping hand in some way to another person. One of the things that motivates us to give that helping hand is empathy. As we "walk in another's shoes" and see what life is like for them, we can often overcome our own prejudices and assumptions about others who might need a helping hand. Empathy overcomes prejudice and allows people to connect in a positive way.

❧

ELIZABETH ANN SETON
(1774–1821)

Who She Was

Elizabeth Ann Seton founded the first American religious community, the Sisters of Charity. She was born into a wealthy society family and raised an Episcopalian. Richard Bayley, her father, taught her to have a spirit of service to others. When Elizabeth was nineteen, she married William Seton, a wealthy businessman. During their marriage, they traveled to Italy, where she witnessed her Catholic friends living out their faith in action. This prompted Elizabeth to convert to Catholicism. As a result, she was rejected by her family, who looked down on Catholics as lower class and ignorant. Tragically, William's business failed and he died, leaving her with five young children and no money.

Elizabeth opened a school for girls in Baltimore, Maryland, in order to support her children and give them an education. The women who worked with her at the school are known today as the Sisters of Charity. She was their Mother Seton. Only forty-seven years old when she died, she is the first person born in the United States to be declared a saint.

Her Life Speaks to Me

Elizabeth Ann Seton's life was one of adjusting to changes so radical that they might have led another person to discouragement and perhaps even to hopelessness. From living the pampered life of a wealthy young woman and then a society matron, she became a poor widow. In addition, she suffered rejection by her family and the death of several of her children. What Elizabeth Ann did in each case was to put her foot on the path that was before her and trust in God while using her own skills and ingenuity. She used her teaching skills and not only supported herself but also helped give young girls the opportunity for education for the first time. She created a new family by surrounding herself with women who shared her same values and passion for service.

Following Her Example

We may not establish a religious order during our lifetime or live the life of a wealthy society person. However, we can identify with Elizabeth Ann Seton by our experience with obstacles, hardships, and unexpected difficulties in our lives. Whatever life puts in our path, we can look to her example of what we are to do. God has given each of us more strength than we know and perhaps many talents that are only unwrapped for us when we are challenged. Like Elizabeth Ann we can trust that if we take one step at a time and ask for God's help we, too, may find resources inside ourselves that will enable us to face whatever tomorrow may bring. A woman of prayer, her life can remind us, that it is often in reaching out to help others that we find our own way.

✠

ELIZABETH OF HUNGARY (1207–1231)

Who She Was

Catholic Charities USA is one of the nation's largest social service networks serving those most in need of care, of food, and of all kinds of human services. It is not surprising that Elizabeth of Hungary is their patron saint, because her dedication of service to those in need so closely mirrors the work of Catholic Charities.

Elizabeth was a queen and a member of the social elite who at a very young age put herself completely at the service of the poor, sick, and homeless. Born in Hungary in 1207, Elizabeth was the daughter of Andrew, King of Hungary. In an arranged marriage in 1221, she wed Louis of Thuringia. They had three children. Elizabeth was widowed when Louis died while fighting in the Crusades.

Even though she was a member of the royal court, she led an austerely simple life and devoted herself to works of charity. The story goes that she constantly gave away her jewels and clothes to the poor. Her husband thought her work with the outcasts was beneath her role as queen. However once, when he demanded to see what she was hiding in her cloak, instead of the food for the poor he expected to find, when she opened the cloak, roses spilled out. According to legend, from then on he shared in her ministry. This is also why Elizabeth is often depicted with a shower of roses in her lap.

Her Life Speaks to Me

A great deal happened to this young woman in the short life she lived: an arranged marriage, a family who did not understand her passion and devotion to service, widowhood. She faced many obstacles at each step of the way. When her husband died, his family apparently had her sent away and she was even homeless for a time. Her choices in life were misunderstood but she kept on doing what she believed in spite of serious obstacles.

Following Her Example

Elizabeth began reaching out to others when she was still very young. Consider the young people whom you know, perhaps those young adults who are already offering their services and could benefit from your encouragement and prayer. Imagine the energy and good will they possess that can be put at the service of those in need. Think about how you might encourage them or even connect them with opportunities to help others. Perhaps contacting your parish staff or your diocesan Catholic Charities can shed light on specific opportunities. If others misunderstand you, be encouraged by Elizabeth's example and do not give in to the pressure to change the path that you have chosen.

✠

FÉLIX VARELA Y MORALES
(1788–1853)

Who He Was

His grandparents in St. Augustine, Florida, raised this complex and brilliant priest after his parents died in his native Cuba. They noticed that Felix was intellectually gifted and took the steps for him to become well educated in his youth. Later on, when he returned to Cuba as a priest, Félix taught in the national seminary for ten years. As a representative of Cuba in Spain's parliament, he joined in a petition drive for Cuba's independence from Spain and the abolition of slavery for black Cubans. When Spain sentenced him to death for these views, he fled into self-exile.

Exile for Félix Varela meant being in New York City at a time when there was great discrimination against the Catholic immigrants moving there. While in New York, he established a church and schools for the immigrants. As Vicar General, his primary pastoral attention was helping these refugees from hunger and poverty. He was a strong advocate for women and worked to establish self-help programs for them. Félix founded the first Spanish-language newspaper in the United States and published many essays on the importance of education and the need for cooperation between the Spanish-speaking and English-speaking communities.

Cuba gives a national award in his name and there is a movement in his native country to promote his cause for canonization as a saint. The U.S. Postal Service issued a commemorative stamp with his picture on it. Félix Varela y Morales, however, was more interested in Catholic immigrants, abolition of slavery, and the independence of Cuba from Spain than any such honors for himself.

His Life Speaks to Me

A man of superior intelligence and outstanding education who enjoyed positions of power and authority in Cuba, Spain, and the Archdiocese of New York, it would not have been surprising for Félix to become arrogant and elitist. The exact opposite is true as Father Félix remained grounded in the mandate of Jesus Christ to care for the poor and vulnerable. He depended on prayer and devotion to the Eucharist as his anchor to keep him tirelessly devoted to helping those who were looked down upon both in Cuba and the United States.

Following His Example

Even if a person never leaves the town where he is born or becomes well educated or powerful, he still can do something to help other people in need. Whether it is saying a daily prayer for the poor and desperate, donating used clothing, helping in a soup kitchen, pressuring politicians to help the needy, or donating money to people overseas in crisis, there are more ways to help now than in Félix's day, and there are many more people who need the kind of care that Christ wants us to provide. Each person can do something each day.

✠

FRANCES CABRINI (1850–1917)

Who She Was

Frances Cabrini was not a woman to sit still for long. She was born and raised in a small village in Italy. She became an American citizen in Seattle, Washington, lived for years in New York City, and died in Chicago. During her lifetime, she crossed the Atlantic Ocean twenty-four times. Her stamina and remarkable accomplishments hide the fact that she was such a sickly person that she was not allowed at first to enter the convent. Frances taught and worked in an orphanage and eventually the sisters there did allow her to join them. When their orphanage closed, Frances organized a new group of missionary sisters, the Missionaries of the Sacred Heart. As missionaries, they sailed to New York to begin what would be the first of sixty-seven institutions (orphanages, hospitals, and schools) in her lifetime. One can only imagine the energy and determination it took to accomplish all Frances Cabrini did.

The first years in New York alone were filled with trials. Arriving without knowing the language, these missionaries upon their arrival found out that those running the house in which they were to stay did not expect them and the building they had been promised as a school was occupied and in need of great repair. These challenges seemed to be par for the course as Frances and the others went about advocating for the immigrants and homeless. She helped found hospitals, orphanages, and schools, and responded to the hungers for food, shelter, and spiritual nourishment of the immigrant communities.

Her Life Speaks to Me

Reading about people who accomplish extraordinary things in their lifetime may seem to put them at such a distance that we cannot even relate to them. However, Frances' human qualities have much to offer as an example of how we can live. She listened to people and learned their stories before she even decided how to help them. Listening is a wonderful quality to imitate. Frances encouraged the people she met to follow their dreams, to do all they could to lift themselves up. She lived with physical difficulties but continued to do what she could; she did not hide behind them or use her poor health as an excuse. Her attitude of "Let's just do it!" helped overcome the many disappointments, changes, and setbacks in life.

Following Her Example

The "saint of the immigrants," as she is sometimes called, would have plenty to keep her busy if Frances lived today. There are many opportunities for us also to reach out to immigrants through our own personal actions or through the many Catholic agencies and organizations ready to help. How we deal with disappointments and problems is an indication of our character and the will to do all we can in this lifetime. Frances offers a wonderful example to us of not hiding behind difficulties as an excuse not to keep on trying but to embrace the attitude of "Let's just do it!"

✦

FRANCIS OF ASSISI (1181–1226)

Who He Was

Imagine growing up the son of a wealthy merchant in the beautiful city of Assisi, Italy. Francis dreamed of being a brave soldier one day. However, his experience was quite different because as a soldier, he ended up becoming a prisoner of war. After being freed a year later, Francis was no longer the person his family had known.

Visiting a church one day, Francis thought the Lord told him to repair the deteriorating building. Francis stole some merchandise from his father, sold it, and tried unsuccessfully to give the money to the parish priest for repairs. Francis' father was furious with him, beat him, and humiliated him in the town square in front of the bishop. Francis gave his father everything he had with him, including his money and his clothes. Leaving home, he went to live among the poor while he tried to rebuild the church with his own hands. Eventually he realized the Lord was calling him not just to repair this particular building but to rebuild the Church itself by preaching the Gospel. Soon others followed him and they were particularly devoted to helping the poor.

In addition, Francis appreciated the beauty of God's creation and all of nature. He is the patron saint for animals and many churches have a blessing of pets and animals on his feast day of October 4.

The Franciscans were beggars, living off what people would give them as they preached and cared for the sick. Today, the Franciscans live and minister all over the world by continuing to imitate Francis' example.

His Life Speaks to Me

Francis was a man who had the courage of his convictions. He discovered his mission in life as a young man and was focused completely on living it out. As an example of humility, courage, and profound trust that God would be with him if he was true to himself, Francis inspired others to look at how they were living their own lives as well.

Following His Example

Each person is created with a particular mission in life. When we discover what that is, why we were born, we can be free to follow that path. No one is created just like another person. No one has the same personality, strengths, and talents. Recognizing our unique gifts helps us discover what God wants of us. When we are clear about our mission, it will influence our personal life, our work, our family life, and our relationships with others because it is the essence of who we are. Talking with someone who knows us well and prayerfully asking God's help, we can name our mission in life and strive to live it.

✠

GIANNA BERETTA MOLLA
(1922–1962)

Who She Was

As many women know, it is not easy to carry out the roles of mother and wife while also working as a professional person. In fact, as the life of Gianna Molla shows, it demands many sacrifices to live what may sound like an ordinary life. Gianna was a doctor who lived in the twentieth century, although at the time she entered the medical profession it was quite unusual for a woman to do so. She was born in Milan, Italy, and her life of forty years was both extraordinary and ordinary. She loved life, especially music, hiking, and skiing.

As a physician, she specialized in pediatrics and opened a medical clinic in Mesero, near Milan, giving special attention to mothers, babies, the elderly, and the poor. She considered medicine her mission in life. Dr. Molla and her husband had three children while she continued her practice. Before the birth of her fourth child, Gianna experienced two miscarriages. She became pregnant again but within a week of the fourth baby's birth, Gianna died of complications from infection and a benign tumor that had complicated her pregnancy. She took care that the life of her unborn child would not be sacrificed for hers.

Her Life Speaks to Me

Gianna is a wonderful example of seeing the holy in the commonplace, the extraordinary in the ordinary. Cardinal Martini explained it this way: "Her life is the same as that of many men and women, made up of little events that don't make the history books. Her capacity for heroism comes from her healthy everyday life, an example of popular holiness that is accessible to everyone." Gianna described what guided her life: "I have always been taught that the secret of happiness is living moment by moment and to thank God for everything that in His goodness He sends us, day after day." Her witness of a generous, loving life doing whatever she was called to do can inspire both men and women who experience conflicting demands in a busy life.

Following Her Example

Gianna had a wonderful and rich understanding of holiness. Like her, we live very ordinary lives for the most part, and our holiness comes from living our life in the spirit of thankfulness for God's goodness each day. Gianna knew what God wanted of her by following her own normal path and using whatever the talents with which she was blessed. In the midst of lives that are often too busy, her thankful prayer to God each day is an example to us of how to be in touch with the source of our own holiness as we live "moment by moment." If we walk through life with our eyes really open, watching and noticing the goodness around us, the holiness in the ordinary, like Gianna we will be living as God wants us to live.

❧

HENRI NOUWEN (1932–1996)

Who He Was

Henri Nouwen wrote dozens of books on the spiritual life along with giving countless talks and conferences. He taught at Notre Dame, Yale, and Harvard. To the thousands of people whose lives he touched, he appeared to have it all: a deep spiritual life, huge success in his profession, worldwide acclaim. It would be a shock to many of them that Henri suffered greatly, felt quite alone, and lived with great anxiety and a need for affection and affirmation. His search for the solution to this restlessness took him in many directions: from academia to a Trappist monastery, to a life with the poor in Latin America, to a period being the caretaker of a severely disabled young man at the L'Arche community in Toronto. He even suffered a severe emotional breakdown in the midst of his search for peace.

Despite his great internal suffering, Henri Nouwen touched countless people with his compassion and his remarkable ability to speak and write of his conviction that the spiritual life is not just for saints or extraordinary people. Christ's call is primarily for ordinary people, those who are not only imperfect but also who, in one way or another, are limping through life. Most people are in need of some kind of healing. Henri believed the call of Christ and the love of God alone can heal. He knew from his own search during a life of restlessness and anxiety that God was there for those who hunger and thirst for love. It was during a time of peace in his life that he suffered a heart attack and died. Ironically, he was traveling through his native Holland to work on a film about the Prodigal Son, his favorite painting. This moment in his own life, too, was about the Father welcoming his son home with great joy and opened arms.

His Life Speaks to Me

Henri Nouwen was extraordinary in so many ways. He was a gifted writer and speaker and he was profoundly insightful in the area of spirituality. Evidently, he was also a fragile person with hungers that even his fame and attention could not satisfy. Like so many people, he was trying to *be* good and to *do* good. Yet Henri was unable for many years to overcome what kept him from being the person he appeared to be. That is why his extraordinary life has such credibility with ordinary people. His life and his writings teach that God is here for ordinary people. As stated repeatedly in the Gospels, Christ came into the world for those who labor and are burdened.

Following His Example

Henri Nouwen continued his search for decades through both good and very difficult times. Regular prayerful conversation with God is the most important of all Henri Nouwen's teachings, and it is a gift that each of us can give ourselves. Never give up the search for the peace that only God can give.

✠

IGNATIUS OF LOYOLA
(1491–1556)

Who He Was

Who would think a cannon ball could have such power and influence! The young soldier Ignatius was undergoing a long and painful recuperation from a war injury caused by a cannon ball that shattered his leg. He was bored and lonely. He decided to read to pass the time and the only reading material available was a life of Christ and the lives of some saints. What he read moved him to put aside his plans to marry a lady of the court in Spain and have a military career. Instead, he began a slow and sometimes interrupted journey toward finding out how God wanted him to live a life in imitation of Christ. Ignatius knew that he needed more education.

During the course of his studies, he discovered his gift for spiritual direction and teaching and began using it while a student. On more than one occasion, the Inquisition imprisoned him for teaching religion without being ordained. Cleared of any irregularities in his teaching, he bonded with a group of six graduate students that included Francis Xavier. This group eventually became the first Jesuits and were later ordained in Venice. Initially, they carried out their ministry in Italy.

During his life as a Jesuit, Ignatius was very interested in the foreign missions. However, the education of youth also developed as a priority in the Jesuit ministry. Today there are Jesuit education centers throughout the world. His Spiritual Exercises continue to be followed today by religious and lay people as well as individuals of many different faiths who follow his Ignatian method of personal prayer.

His Life Speaks to Me

"All for the greater glory of God" (*Ad Majorem Dei Gloriam*) was the motto by which Ignatius lived. Since the beginning, it has been the motto of the Jesuits also. Whatever is done is done for the glory of God. Ignatius obviously accomplished extraordinary things, but his goal was to do everything for the glory of God, not for himself. He was called to do only things that would give glory, not shame, to his Creator. One of the significant ways he accomplished this was to make daily prayer essential in his life. The prayer of Ignatius used all the senses as well as the memory and the mind in quiet conversation with God.

Following His Example

The gift that every person can choose to accept from St. Ignatius is the practice of daily prayer. Taking time to begin each day with an awareness of God's presence beside us and within us can shape how we approach each person and each situation. Taking time to look back over the day in quiet examination is a simple but important method to keeping one's life on track. Taking time out for reflective reading of scripture or retreat brings us closer to living by the motto of Ignatius, *Ad Majorem Dei Gloriam*!

⬦

ISAAC HECKER (1819–1888)

Who He Was

Evangelization, proclaiming the Good News of Jesus Christ, is an emphasis in the Church today. Isaac Hecker, who founded the Paulist Fathers more than one hundred and fifty years ago, is the model of American Catholic evangelization. Isaac was born in New York City of German immigrant parents. As a young boy of eleven, Isaac had to leave school to work in the family bakery business. This was one of many changes in his life along an unusual and fruitful path. As a young man, he embarked on a spiritual search that took him in many directions. Even as a teenager, he sometimes gave street speeches on political and social topics. Eventually he became a Catholic. His preaching led him to many places and took on many different forms.

When Isaac joined the Redemptorist community, he studied in Belgium, did parish work briefly in England, then returned to America and preached with a mission band of Redemptorists. European immigration to the United States was at its height at that time in the nineteenth century. The Redemptorists preached to and served these people, who often faced hostility because of their religion. Isaac excelled at helping immigrant Catholics see how well their faith fit in with their new culture.

Isaac Hecker was such a powerful lecturer and preacher on the Catholic faith that he was invited to preach in many cities. It was never an easy road for him. When a misunderstanding arose between the American branch of the Redemptorists and their European superiors, Father Hecker went to Rome to represent the Americans. However, as things turned out, he was actually expelled from his community. Pope Pius IX encouraged him and his companions to form a new religious community in 1858. As a result, Father Hecker is often credited with the founding of the first American religious community.

The Missionary Society of St. Paul, or more commonly known as the Paulist Fathers, continues the mission of evangelization begun by Isaac Hecker to help teach both Catholics and others about the Catholic faith tradition. The initial communication forms of preaching and printing have been expanded to using the media of the contemporary to preach the Gospel message to spiritual seekers like Isaac Hecker.

His Life Speaks to Me

Isaac Hecker was a searcher and this resulted in finding his spiritual home in the Catholic faith. He recognized the talents God gave him and made use of the skills of speech and communication as fully as he could. He faced difficulties as a child, great challenges and obstacles as a member of a religious order, and personal suffering at the end of his life. Yet he persevered and experienced even greater opportunities to make use of his God-given talents, spreading the word through the community he founded.

Following His Example

Prayer and honest searching can enable each person to recognize his or her God-given talents. We are most effective when we honor and use those talents in the important areas of our lives. Very few people go through life without challenges and obstacles. Like Isaac Hecker, we are doing God's will if we trust and persevere on the path God has given us to walk in this lifetime.

JANE FRANCES DE CHANTAL (1572–1641)

Who She Was

This wealthy young woman lived in a French castle and oversaw the servants and the entire estate while her husband, a baron, served in the king's army. The kitchen was always open with soup and bread ready for the beggars who would come each day. Then tragedy struck. Her husband, Christophe, was killed in a hunting accident and Jane and her three children were left alone. Their lives changed dramatically. They were suddenly poor when her elderly father-in-law refused to let them keep any property or money, and they were forced to live a difficult life with him and his resentful housekeeper.

During these years, Jane herself taught the children to read and write as well as to learn the catechism. She went to church where she heard the bishop Francis de Sales preach. He became her spiritual director and they were friends for many years. Francis wanted to start a religious order for widows. Jane put off her decision to join such a group until her daughters were married and her son in his teens.

The vision of Jane and Francis was to start a community for women who would divide their time between work and prayer, going out to visit the poor and caring for the sick. However, the Church officials at that time disagreed with this new idea and their community of Visitation nuns were a cloistered order. At the time of her death in 1641, there were more than eighty convents of Visitation Sisters. St. Vincent de Paul described Jane Frances de Chantal as one of the holiest people he ever met.

Her Life Speaks to Me

Jane's life looks very successful at first glance. She raised a family and later began a religious order. However, throughout her life she faced a great many hardships. Her husband died and she lived a difficult life as a widow. She was disappointed greatly because her religious sisters were not allowed to minister outside the convent. Her son was killed, the plague in France resulted in the death of her daughter-in-law and son-in-law, and her friend Francis de Sales died. Jane was always a devout woman but suffered great doubts of faith through the years. Like many of us today, Jane had struggles throughout her life.

Following Her Example

There are times when life brings serious difficulties that may even seem hopeless. Perhaps it may be people dear to us who are seriously ill or die, relationships that disappoint and hurt us, or major family problems that cause pain. Our faith may seem elusive and difficult. Jane's struggle with her faith offers us a wonderful example of getting up each day and putting one foot in front of the other. We will survive and even thrive with God's help, just as she did.

✠

JOHN HENRY NEWMAN (1801–1890)

Who He Was

Born in England during the Victorian era, John Henry Newman was an Anglican priest, theologian, and writer. He was a traditionalist who also valued dialogue with the modern world, and Newman spent a good deal of his life at Oxford University, first as a student, then as a teacher, and later as vicar of its University Church of St. Mary. He was a leader in the conservative Oxford movement but he was later denounced, which caused him to leave to write a history of Christian doctrine. This research led him to become a Roman Catholic and eventually a priest. Initially however, he was not well received. Newman joined the order of St. Philip Neri and went to a working-class city to establish an Oratory there. Later, in Dublin, he established a Catholic university and it was here that he wrote his classic volume, *The Idea of a University*. Pope Leo XIII named him a cardinal.

John Henry Newman lived at a time when there were serious divisions in the Catholic Church between groups that identified themselves as conservatives and liberals. He was troubled by the authoritarian manner among the hierarchy of his time. In 1859, he wrote "On Consulting the Laity in Matters of Faith." As a man who lived in tension between the modern world and tradition, Cardinal Newman stood for having a real understanding of the history of doctrine. He defended the role of the laity and believed in the separation of church and state and the rights of conscience. While Cardinal Newman may have felt at home in the post-Vatican II Church, he sensed being out of step in his time.

His Life Speaks to Me

One of the first things many people notice about John Henry Newman is that he continued to learn about his faith. This desire brought him into conflict with beliefs he had always held and eventually led him into the Catholic Church. Such a move takes courage. Though not well accepted in his new religious denomination, his informed conscience was what he followed even when others disagreed with him. He learned about the history of tradition and greatly valued it. In turn, this helped open his eyes and made him a person who was deeply committed.

Following His Example

"I'm too busy" is sometimes the excuse people use for not continuing to learn about their faith. How we spend our time is often an indicator of what we value and what we consider as important in our lifetime. Reading about other saints and models of holiness is a good way to continue to learn and to deepen our faith. Continuing to learn about our faith, searching for understanding, and being committed in religious tradition gives us the courage to speak and act according to the will of God, which we discover by better informing our conscience and ourselves.

✢

POPE JOHN XXIII (1881–1963)

Who He Was

Pope John XXIII chose his papal name to honor two men named John who served as models for his priesthood: John, the disciple of love and John the Baptist, the herald of Christ. The world was surprised when John XXIII was elected, yet in his short time as pope he had a powerful effect on the Church and on the world.

Born in the northern part of Italy, Angelo Giuseppe Roncalli was one of nine children born to poor tenant farmers. During his life, he never lost sight of the importance of remembering and reaching out to those who had less than most and those who struggled to make a living. In one of his letters, he reminded his family that humility, poverty, and happiness are better than pride, ambition, and pursuing wealth.

In his seminary years and later as a priest, Angelo spent time in military duty. Father Roncalli taught in the seminary and during World War II used his diplomatic skills in troubled areas of Europe. As pope, he became an outspoken advocate for peace during a dangerous time in history. He wrote to the president of France that war is a return to barbarism and ruins civilization. He is credited with doing much to prevent a third world war. Throughout all of his challenging positions, he was known for his mildness, tranquility, humor, and openness to reach out to the world beyond the Church.

Pope John XXIII is primarily remembered for his role in convening the Second Vatican Council. His stated goal of opening the windows of the Church enlivened many and frightened others. He is seen as responsible for changing the face of Roman Catholicism, making its ancient roots and beliefs alive again, and allowing the liturgy to be understood and prayed by all worshippers. During the Council's opening session, Pope John XXIII was suffering with cancer. His pontificate was five short years and he died before the second session of the Vatican Council reconvened. Nevertheless, this holy and profoundly pastoral leader left a lasting mark on the Church he loved so well.

His Life Speaks to Me

This pope never let any of his accomplishments or honors affect who he was. As pope, he continued to visit hospitals, prisons, and churches in Rome, realizing the importance of staying in touch with all the people. His large extended family had its own ongoing problems and he continued to walk with them in their challenges. He was as surprised as the rest of the world that he was elected pope and never lost his sense of humor. However, he used the great gifts God had given him to lead courageously even in the face of opposition.

Following His Example

In one of his daily messages, Pope John XXIII wrote that the Lord calls every person. The important thing, he said, is that we find out how we are to answer that call. John listened for the call. In our own life, we can do the same. He never planned or even imagined the roles and challenges he would face, but he carried them out with genuine earnestness and humility and did not waste the talents and gifts he possessed. We are each to respond to the calls in our life in the same way: with humility, making good use of the gifts we are blessed with, and always being clear that our talents are from the Lord.

⬧

JOSEPH BERNARDIN
(1928–1996)

Who He Was

A Catholic couple from northern Italy came to the United States and settled in Charleston, South Carolina. Years later, their son, Joseph, would visit his mother every day in the nursing home in Chicago until he himself died. This son grew up wanting to be a medical doctor. However, he changed paths in college and entered the seminary. That decision led him in a new direction that included many moves from parish priest in Charleston, to working at the United States Conference of Catholic Bishops in Washington, D.C., to becoming archbishop in Cincinnati and subsequently cardinal in Chicago. He was the point person in the 1983 U.S. Bishops' Pastoral Letter, *The Challenge of Peace*, which strongly condemned nuclear war and was critical of U.S. military policies.

One of his major contributions was the "Seamless Garment" position that he wrote and spoke about at great length. This position on viewing all forms of life as sacred dealt with the issues of abortion, capital punishment, euthanasia, and concern for the poor and vulnerable in society. During his time in Chicago, he began the Common Ground initiative to bring the conservative and progressive elements of the Church into conversation with each other.

At the suggestion of his priests, he became much more focused on Christ in his life rather than Church administration. This served him well during a personal crisis in which a seminarian accused him of sexual abuse during the time when Cardinal Bernardin was in Ohio. This public humiliation lasted until the man withdrew his charges and apologized. Subsequently, the two men privately met in a time of forgiveness and reconciliation. Shortly afterward, Cardinal Bernardin was diagnosed with pancreatic cancer. During this time of illness, he spent more time in his "priestly" ministry and became the "unofficial chaplain" to Chicago cancer patients. When he died on November 14, 1996, more than one hundred thousand prayer cards were distributed to people who came to pay their respects to this beloved Church leader.

His Life Speaks to Me

Cardinal Bernardin was the first to offer a Mass for divorced and separated Catholics at Holy Name Cathedral. He also set up a task force to ensure that the Archdiocese of Chicago offered care for those stricken by AIDS. One Protestant minister remarked upon Cardinal Bernardin's death, "He could listen to people and make you believe that you were being heard and taken seriously, even if you didn't necessarily believe he would change his mind because of what you said."

Following His Example

The need for forgiveness and reconciliation permeates our world today. It is needed in our families, neighborhoods, and parishes as well. The challenge of a publicly false personal accusation may not be a common experience for many. However, if each person would seek and offer forgiveness to one person who has offended them or ask forgiveness of another whose forgiveness they need, it could change the atmosphere of our world. Joseph Bernardin carried the Prayer of St. Francis of Assisi with him, which begins with the words, "Lord, make me an instrument of your peace." Every person can find ways to become instruments of peace. It can begin with sincere and open listening as well as really hearing what the other person is saying.

✦

JOSEPHINE BAKHITA (1869–1947)

Who She Was

The life of Josephine Bakhita reads like a story someone imagined. Born in Sudan, south of Egypt, Bakhita lived in a simple hut with her happy and loving family in the southwestern part of the country. She and her twin sister had three brothers and three sisters. Although they lived in a typical mud hut, hired servants worked the family plantation and took care of the cattle. One day when she was seven years old, she was kidnapped by slave traders. Her life became a nightmare. She was forced to march long distances in slave caravans. The slave traders gave her the name, Bakhita, which ironically means "the lucky one." Over a period of ten years, she was sold four times. Her owners beat her, sometimes until she lost consciousness. One of them had her body cut sixty times for decorations or "tattoos."

Bakhita's life turned a corner when an Italian family living in Africa purchased her. They returned to Italy with her and treated her well. Eventually, as the nanny of an Italian child, she accompanied the girl to the Canossian Sisters in Venice where Bakhita came to know about God for the first time. She was amazed at what she learned. Later she said that all her life she had experienced God in her heart without knowing Him because of the beautiful things in nature: the sun, the moon, and the stars. She felt that someone must be the master of these amazing things. Eventually Bakhita received the Sacraments of Christian Initiation and took the name Josephine when she joined the convent there. For another fifty years, as a Daughter of Charity, she lived in the community in Schio cooking, sewing, and welcoming the poor. People in Vicena, Italy, called her "our Black Mother."

A woman of enormous forgiveness, Josephine never harbored anger and revenge toward the people who had kidnapped her, tortured her, and kept her a slave. Josephine always kept hope alive in her heart no matter the circumstances and did not allow herself to be bitter at what life had brought her.

Her Life Speaks to Me

Forgiveness, hope, and a lack of bitterness at the unfairness of life are qualities with which most people can relate.

Life is unfair, especially when people treat us badly. However, the hope that comes from the well of our Christian faith can help us follow, even in a small way, the path that Josephine Bakhita models for us.

Following Her Example

The need to forgive and to be forgiven touches every human life. Sometimes people need to forgive others. Sometimes the same person needs to ask for forgiveness. Overcoming pride or other obstacles is worth the effort for the wonderful experience of inner peace that forgiveness often brings. Very often, the greatest need is to forgive oneself for something in the past. Josephine's extraordinary life can serve as an example for us of this great liberating experience of forgiveness.

✦

JULIAN OF NORWICH (1342–1420)

Who She Was

In the twenty-first century, our lives are filled with busyness, with people, and often with more activities than we might want to have. Julian, in contrast, lived in total prayerful solitude in a room attached to a church in the fourteenth century. What could we possibly learn from her? Surprisingly, quite a bit!

Little is know of this remarkable person. Even her name is uncertain, but it may be taken from the church—St. Julian of Norwich, in England—where she lived. While her lifestyle may seem odd and escapist to us, in her day it was considered an important social function rather than a rejection of the world.

Julian was a woman of great compassion and love. We discover this in her writings, for which she is most famous. During a period in which she was extremely ill and thought to be dying, she received a number of revelations or "showings." Over many years following this experience she wrote what these visions taught, in her book, *Showings*.

The image of God people had in Julian's time was of a God of anger and of judgment over a sinful world. The Inquisition was at full force rooting out heresy. Julian, however, was entirely positive, focusing on divine grace and not on the errors of God's creatures. In her revelations, the cross is a sign of consolation, and her visions stressed that life was striving for virtue out of love for God. She also emphasized her "direct approach" to God.

At the time, the Eucharist was celebrated in a way in which the faithful attended but rarely participated in or received communion. Julian, in contrast, referred to the Eucharist as Christ feeding his children with Himself and it was not to be refused. She appreciated the world as good and said that she was told, "God made it, God loves it, God keeps it."

Her Life Speaks to Me

Julian's example teaches us, among other things, that having a healthy and deep spiritual life does not depend on being highly educated. It is primarily about staying in conversation with God. She spent time listening to the voice of God in her heart even though it was quite different from the religious customs and theology of the times. Julian stepped away from the negative image of God that church leaders and the common piety of the day stressed and trusted in Christ and what she herself learned from her relationship with God.

Following Her Example

We, too, can "go to God" our own way. Staying in conversation with God, as Julian teaches, is precisely what prayer is. Real prayer is communication with God; we speak what is in our heart. We can each listen to the voice of God in our heart and act on what we learn. We can follow Julian's conviction about the Eucharist and participate fully in this source and summit of our faith rather than making it a time of private prayer. The celebration of the Eucharist is not for us to hide away from the world but to be engaged in it, treasuring it as God's creation to be cared for and honored.

✦

KARL RAHNER (1904–1984)

Who He Was

A quiet man, Karl Rahner was raised in a traditional Catholic family in Freiburg, Germany. To some, his life may have appeared to be fairly routine, even monotonous. As a Jesuit he taught, wrote, and served as a pastoral minister. However, God gave him the gift of a great intellect that enabled him to become quite learned in studying philosophy and theology. His life's work was devoted to bringing human life in conversation and relationship with God.

God, he stressed, is closer to us and deeper within our daily existence than most of us ever realize. Our religious experience is not something separate from our humanity. Grace, which is God's self-communication to us, is not something "out there" and poured into us from afar. God is always with us and reaches out to us in every situation in our life. It is up to us to open ourselves to this gift.

Karl Rahner wrote and taught what he believed. However, some church officials severely criticized him and eventually his works had to be submitted to a censor. In time, his brilliant insights and love for truth were recognized and honored. He was named by John XXIII to be a theological expert at the Second Vatican Council, where his theological thoughts and pastoral insights had great influence that still continues today.

His Life Speaks to Me

A man of remarkable gifts and accomplishments, it might be surprising that Rahner's self-assessment was very humble and modest. When asked about his accomplishments, which included more than sixteen hundred publications bearing his name, Karl Rahner said, "I worked, wrote, taught, tried to do my duty, and earned my living. I tried in this ordinary everyday way to serve God—that's it."

Karl Rahner was an ordinary man who "put on the shoes" of everyday living going about the tasks of his work. He used whatever God gave him and accepted what life brought his way, whether the suffering of severe criticism or the adulation of success. His humility was not without courage. His courage was born of his faithful belief that God is intimately with us every step of the way.

Following His Example

When we find ourselves being criticized by others, we can follow his example by seriously examining what we are doing, testing whether the criticism is valid, and then continuing on whatever path we choose with humility, confident that God is with us. As Karl Rahner believed, it is up to us to open ourselves to the gift of God's presence. We do this by reminding ourselves daily of this amazing reality. Like him, our life may seem quite ordinary, but it is important to remember that life is about trying to do God's will. As Karl Rahner taught, we can be assured that God is with us every step of the way.

✠

KATERI TEKAKWITHA
(1656–1680)

Who She Was

Kateri Tekakwitha was born in 1656 in New York state. While several places claim to be her birthplace, it is commonly thought that she was born in what is now called Auriesville. Kateri's father was a Mohawk and her mother an Algonquin. When she was four years old, a smallpox epidemic killed both her parents and her baby brother. She herself was physically scarred with pockmarks on her face and left nearly blind from the smallpox. Her two aunts and her uncle, who was also a Mohawk and chief of the Turtle clan, took her in to live with them.

Kateri learned of Christianity at about eleven years old when some missionaries stayed in her uncle's lodge for several days. The missionaries had been part of a group negotiating peace between the French and Mohawks in Quebec. The girl eagerly listened to them and accepted their message in her heart. It was some time later than the Turtle clan relocated near the village of Fonda, New York. Kateri decided to be baptized; she made her way to the village and was baptized there. This conversion set her at serious odds with her family, who did not accept her religion. Because she considered Sunday her Christian "day of rest," they refused to give her food on that day. The opposition to her faith became so intense that finally her uncle's lodge ceased to be a place of protection to her.

Kateri felt she needed to escape and live with people who accepted her faith. With the help of some other Native Americans, during the course of more than two months she walked two hundred miles north through woods, rivers, and swamps to the Canadian Jesuit mission of St. Francis Xavier near Montreal. She spent the last three years of her life there and died at the age of twenty-four. Blessed Kateri Tekakwitha is the patroness of ecology and the environment.

Her Life Speaks to Me

It is not an uncommon experience for young people having to make a decision that goes against the group. In fact, it is not uncommon for people of any age. However, few people would have a challenge like young Kateri, to choose to be a Christian in the midst of a family and village that was violently opposed. Her courage extended to setting off to live elsewhere by walking through the wilderness in the northern woods. The trek itself would demand courage. Yet, in spite of all she went through, this strong young orphan is remembered primarily for her serenity in the midst of a life of remarkable hardship.

Following Her Example

Where do we find peace and serenity? Kateri gives us a wonderful example of the power of faith. Her faith was her anchor. Her faith gave her courage. Her faith was the basis for the hallmark of serenity for which she was admired. Anchored in our faith, we too can have the courage to go against what others are doing when we know it is not what God wants of us. Like Kateri, we can rely on our faith to be a rich source of peace and serenity for us. However, the flower of faith needs to be nurtured. We are challenged to take the time to acquire the virtue of faith-based serenity that is ours if we want it.

⚬

KATHERINE DREXEL (1858–1955)

Who She Was

As a young adult in Philadelphia, Pennsylvania, Katherine Drexel inherited millions of dollars. Inspired by her banker father, who had been a prayerful person, and by a stepmother who had opened their home several days a week to feed whoever came to the door, Katherine chose an amazing path for her life. She gave away the millions of dollars she inherited from her wealthy parents.

Katherine saw that there were two groups of Americans who were terribly neglected and in need: Native Americans and African Americans. It was to these two groups that she devoted her resources and eventually her life. Beginning with endowing dozens of schools on Native American reservations, she learned that there were no missionaries to serve these groups. This resulted in her founding the Sisters of the Blessed Sacrament for Indians and Colored People. Almost immediately, there were ten sisters in the community. Wealthy as she was, the sisters were not to use her money for themselves but to use it for the education and care of these two groups.

Over the years, she established one hundred and forty-five Catholic missions, twelve schools for Native Americans, and fifty schools for African American students, including Xavier University in New Orleans. It was not unusual for the religious sisters of her community to experience threats and harassment by the Ku Klux Klan. When her sisters described how they were jeered and called names when they participated in Civil Rights marches, Katherine simply asked, "Did you pray for them?"

Her Life Speaks to Me

Here is a preeminent example of someone who reached out to those who are looked down on in our society. Just as her stepmother welcomed the stranger, as Christ taught, Katherine not only welcomed the stranger to her door but she sought out the stranger in the far corners of the country. She went well outside of her comfort zone to do what she felt the Gospel called for as she traveled to reservations, to poor areas of the south, to the western part of our country, and to the slums of the city where she lived. Educated and wealthy, she herself was not impressed by people simply because of what they had or did not have. In fact, she chose to live as though she had nothing, literally giving her treasures to the more needy.

Following Her Example

How difficult it sometimes is not to judge people by how they look! The person on the street who is dirty, someone from another country who looks different and speaks another language or with an accent, people from another religious faith tradition that we do not understand, or someone who speaks as though they are not educated are just a few examples of this way of judging others. We may not be able to work for the betterment of others as Katherine did, but we can certainly strive to become better ourselves with our own openness and welcoming, nonjudgmental attitude. Looking at her life unencumbered by the trappings of wealth, we can develop the habit of asking the question, "Do I need this or simply want this?" when we are adding to our own possessions. We know what Katherine Drexel would answer.

MAISIE WARD (1889–1975)

Who She Was

Maisie Ward was a richly talented woman whose background did not foretell the risks she chose to take all her life. Born in 1889 to a wealthy family of writers in

England, she, too, initially became a writer. However, Maisie heard that Catholic laypeople were preaching in London and she wanted to be part of this. So she left her writing career and joined a movement called the Catholic Evidence Guild. At that time, with no television or Internet, the venue used by many public debaters was Hyde Park in London. The Guild members would go there on Sundays not to debate but to preach publicly the message of Christ and the love of God to anyone who would listen.

As a result of this involvement, Maisie met and married a young Australian, Frank Sheed. Eventually they continued their preaching in a different way. They founded a Catholic book publishing company, Sheed and Ward, which published young, highly talented Catholic writers. They took another risk moving to New York during the Great Depression and published the writings of the Church's leading minds of the day. Maisie eventually began writing again and became the acclaimed author of biographies of saints, martyrs, and Catholic thinkers. Maisie and Frank's motivation was that they "could not sleep while millions were starved of food Christ meant them to have."

That food went beyond the Good News and included both education and the food needed for physical survival. Maisie was vocally critical of the poor quality of some Catholic schools and worked to change that reality. Through her speaking and writing, she raised funds for the poor, organized the Catholic Housing Aid society in England's poor neighborhoods, and raised funds for the poor in India. Dorothy Day reported that at her friend Maisie's death, the church was filled with long, long lines of people whose lives were touched by her preaching and good works.

Her Life Speaks to Me

Maisie believed in the leadership of the laity and never waited for the church leaders to take up a cause where she saw a need. She used her talents to make a difference both directly and indirectly in the mission of spreading God's word through speaking, writing, and publishing voices she felt needed to be heard. In spite of her early wealth, she was greatly sensitive to the needs of the poor and used every means available to her to help those in need.

Following Her Example

Our voice may not be as far-reaching as was Maisie Ward's but we can still use it to speak out for the causes we see as critical to our mission. We can speak through our donations of time and talent perhaps in writing letters to the newspaper, volunteering on phone banks of an organization, asking our priests to preach on critical causes, helping with community organizing projects, or, as Maisie and Frank did, speaking daily in prayer for the strength and insight to do what is right.

❧

MARGARET OF SCOTLAND (1046–1093)

Who She Was

Margaret and her husband, Malcolm, ruled Scotland as king and queen for twenty-three years during the eleventh century. They were married when Margaret's own royal family fled to Scotland at the time the Normans conquered England. In some ways, theirs was an unlikely marriage. He was rough, warlike, and short-tempered, and Margaret was a cultured English princess. She was twenty-four and he nearly forty. Malcolm continued to focus on war and the invasion of England while back in Scotland Margaret's priorities focused on raising the low level of education throughout the country, bringing civility and beauty to the court and the culture, and promoting the arts.

Margaret had a great effect on her husband and he joined in her "hands-on" care for the poor. They would personally feed crowds of the poor, never refusing to help beggars. In fact, statues of Margaret show her with coins in her hand to give to a beggar. Margaret and Malcolm became known as a couple that prayed together. Over the course of time, their example of concern for the poor had a great effect on the country. It is said they "kept two Lents," the usual one before Easter and another before Christmas.

With her husband's help, she founded several churches and used her position and power to address abuses in the Church at that time such as simony (the buying and selling of religious offices or spiritual benefits). She argued strongly for restoring the practice of receiving communion frequently. Margaret died just a few days after her husband was killed in 1093. The policies she initiated brought about a golden age for Scotland that lasted for two hundred years.

Her Life Speaks to Me

Margaret was a blessing for all the people of Scotland. Before she came, there was great ignorance; Margaret worked hard to obtain good teachers, to correct evil practices, and to have new churches built. She was a woman of prayer, a woman who used whatever she had to right the wrongs she saw.

Following Her Example

We can follow Margaret's example of making prayer a part of our daily life, whether or not we imitate any other part of her life. This is particularly true of the Eucharist. Margaret realized the primary importance of the Eucharist in the lives of laypeople and did all she could to help make it widely available. We are following Margaret when we, too, value this great prayer of thanksgiving as the focus of our community and take every opportunity to receive the body and blood of Christ as Jesus asked us to at the Last Supper. Margaret was able to improve education for all in a major way because of her great influence. We can do our own part by valuing our own education and taking advantage of every opportunity to learn, knowing that many people in the world would love to have such a gift. We can use the gift of education we have received by volunteering as a tutor or mentor for those who need our encouragement.

✦

MARTIN DE PORRES (1579–1639)

Who He Was

Born in Lima, Peru, Martin de Porres was the son of a Spanish knight and a woman from Panama. His father, Don Juan, abandoned the family because his children were born black. As a young man, Martin learned how to care for the sick and especially helped the poor. Martin joined the Third Order of Dominicans and asked for the most menial jobs. He worked in the laundry room and on the farm and spent hours in prayer. Some of the Dominican friars at that time thought he should not be allowed in the order because he was black. Martin remained kind to them in spite of their treatment of him.

When he was placed in charge of the sick friars, he was very good in caring for them, staying with them, comforting them, and praying with them. Eventually the community came to respect him to the point that some of the friars asked Martin to be their spiritual director. Word spread of his care for the sick and townspeople began to come to him when they were sick. Martin would care for the sick and injured wherever he found them.

Martin started a home for babies whose parents were too poor to care for them. Wealthy people contributed money to the needy because of him. Eventually he had an influence on many people, rich and poor. He had a special ministry to abandoned African slaves, giving them food and drink as well as tending to those who were sick. When he died, the whole city of Lima mourned his death.

His Life Speaks to Me

Martin de Porres experienced extreme and painful discrimination because of his race from his father, society, and even some members in his religious order. He could easily have grown from an angry child into a bitter man. It is amazing that the total opposite is what he did. As a child, he helped his family survive. As a man, he was certainly the opposite of bitter. His forgiveness of others is extraordinary. What we do not see on the surface of his story is the humility with which he lived. He was not ashamed nor was he arrogant. Rather, he deliberately chose to live humbly both in his physical quarters and in the way he lived, not flaunting his skills in medicine and healing. His extraordinary commitment to daily prayer supported him and rewarded him throughout his life.

Following His Example

Martin de Porres offers much for us to emulate in our own lives. We can examine our attitude towards anyone different–race, religion, sexual orientation, or economic status–and see if we treat them as Martin's father and confreres treated him. We can consciously strive to be the opposite at every opportunity, giving example to others by our words and actions in public. When life treats us unfairly, as it certainly did Martin, we can look to him for a model of forgiveness and lack of bitterness. Like Martin, we can have support for our hardships and encouragement to do the right thing by attending to our prayer life each day.

✠

MAXIMILLIAN MARIA KOLBE (1894–1941)

Who He Was

"I will take his place." With these words, Maximillian Kolbe went to his death by starvation and eventual injection of carbolic acid in a Nazi prison in 1941. This was the usual punishment for another prisoner's escape. Kolbe had volunteered to replace a fellow prisoner, a young father sentenced to die.

A Franciscan priest, Maximillian returned to his native Poland in 1939 after spending time studying in Rome, Japan, and India, where he began publications honoring Mary. As a young man, Maximillian suffered recurring bouts of tuberculosis, which kept him confined from time to time. As a child, he was mischievous and may be described as wild.

That side of his personality did not subside in his adult life. He was sometimes considered very difficult to work with and his superiors would have to remove him from his assignment. A martyr and saint, even his canonization was not without controversy due to anti-Semitism in some of his writings and publications. His monastery, however, was a refugee camp for some fifteen hundred Jews and his death was at the hands of the Nazis in their prison in Auschwitz.

His Life Speaks to Me

"The most deadly poison of our time is indifference," wrote Maximillian Kolbe. He himself certainly was not indifferent. His reputation as a difficult person is an indication that he had the courage of his convictions. He would speak up about his opinions and ideas. Granted, because of this characteristic he was considered difficult, but his refusal to stay silent shows that not only was he not indifferent, but he was passionate about what he believed important. His last human act of self-sacrifice is the ultimate price to pay for not being indifferent, for caring, and for acting on his beliefs.

Following His Example

Maximillian Kolbe is literally a model of the Gospel verse, "Greater love than this no man has than to lay down his life for another." Very few people die for another person. Yet each one of us has things we need to die to. We may need to die to being self-focused in our lives, or die to our desire to acquire things, or die to our perfectionism or laziness. Maximillian's quotation about the poison of indifference challenges us in a more positive direction. We can look at signs of our own indifference. We can discover ways to use our energy less on ourselves and more for others.

Is there a friend or relative who needs a sympathetic ear, or a child who might be helped by some time with me? Am I so overwhelmed hearing about tragedies around the world that I have become indifferent to the needs of those far away? Perhaps I could die to my fear of speaking up so that others in my family or church also become less indifferent to the needs of the hidden homeless in our midst. If we think about it, there are many ways to imitate Maximillian Kolbe in our own life.

⬦

MOLLIE ROGERS (1882–1955)

Who She Was

"Women can be missionaries, too" was the conviction that energized young Mollie Rogers to seek out a priest who was establishing a missionary society for American men. From the time of her first meeting with Father James Walsh in 1905 until her death in 1955, Mollie's dream blossomed into eleven hundred women serving in the Maryknoll Society as missionaries around the world. Interestingly, Mollie's dream was first energized when, as a college student at Smith College, she attended an enthusiastic rally for young Protestant women volunteering to go to China as missionaries. There was no such opportunity for Catholic women and Mollie wished there were. In fact, she was convinced there should be! The idea percolated and grew within her until her meetings with Father Walsh later when she was an instructor at Smith College.

Mollie's vision of women as real missionaries was difficult for the Vatican to accept. The life that she described, of the sisters being out among the people and not behind the cloister, was greatly feared. It was felt that this type of life would be too difficult for them. Eventually her persistence paid off and within a year of the Vatican's approval, there were more than twenty women, now known as the Maryknoll Sisters of St. Dominic.

Mollie became known by her religious name, Mother Mary Joseph. The sisters began by initially working among the Japanese immigrants on the West coast of the United States and eventually became known all over the world. Their focus was on service to the needy, rather than converting people to Catholicism. Conversion, however, so often followed due to their extraordinary example of care as they chose to work among the poorest of the poor. In a great irony, Mollie (Mother Mary Joseph) never got to the missions herself. She spent her entire life at the motherhouse organizing and directing the Maryknoll Sisters' work. Others carried out her dream.

Her Life Speaks to Me

Mollie was obviously a woman of extraordinary talent and great energy, which served her well in overcoming the obstacles in the way of her vision and in directing the huge project that it eventually came to be. Mollie is an amazing example of sacrificing one's personal dream so that others who follow can have an opportunity. Although she never went to the missions as she hoped, countless children and adults received loving care and life-giving service at the hands of hundreds of Maryknoll women because of Mollie's sacrifice.

Following Her Example

Mollie did what many generations of parents have done. She paved the way for the next generations to have opportunities that she did not have. This kind of self-sacrifice is usually rewarded only with the personal satisfaction of making things better for others. Parents sacrifice so their children can have a better education; mothers go without food so that their children can eat; fathers hold down two jobs to make things better. Each one of us can find the place where we will do our part so that the world is better because of our life. It likely will not be in the far-reaching way of Mollie's, but in a quiet, probably unnoticed manner, we will know that we have done all we could.

⚜

MOTHER TERESA (1910–1997)

Who She Was

"There is only one God and He is God to all; therefore it is important that everyone is seen as equal before God. I've always said we should help a Hindu become a better Hindu, a Muslim become a better Muslim, and a Catholic become a better Catholic." These words were spoken by an Albanian, which was a minority group in Slavic Macedonia, a woman who left her country and joined a group of Irish nuns, who themselves eventually became part of the minority group of Roman Catholics in Calcutta, India. This conviction of Mother Teresa's was born of the experience of knowing many different kinds of people in such a deep way that she understood the sacredness of respect for all people. By the time she died in 1997, Agnes Gonxha Bojaxhiu (Mother Teresa) was known, honored, and claimed by many groups around the world.

Her father died when she was young and Agnes immigrated to Ireland to join the convent. The Irish Sisters of Loreto sent her to their high school, St. Mary's, in Calcutta, India, where she taught from 1932 to 1948. The girls in the high school were from wealthy families of all religions. Over the years, Agnes became painfully aware that outside the school walls were huge slums of poor, ill, starving, and needy people.

For two years, she worked on her own as a laywoman. Volunteers helped her start an open-air school for children in the slum. She begged for financial support and the scope of her work grew. After a few years, Agnes received permission from the Holy See to start a community of nuns and became Mother Teresa. The sisters would not wear religious habits but would in every way identify with the people they served, wearing the sari of the poor women and living simply on food they begged. These Missionaries of Charity had as their primary work to love and care for those persons nobody was prepared to look after. Today the order comprises active and contemplative branches of sisters and brothers in many countries.

Her Life Speaks to Me

Mother Teresa followed basic principles in her life that all of us want to live by: acceptance of all people, care for the poor, struggle to be joyful during the many times she had doubts of faith, humility in receiving so many honors. Two of her quotes are enough to fill our every day:

"Keep the joy of loving God in your heart and share this joy with all you meet, especially your family."

"When a poor person dies of hunger, it has not happened because God did not take care of him or her. It has happened because neither you nor I wanted to give that person what he or she needed."

Following Her Example

Copy Mother Teresa's two quotations in a place you will see them each day. Choose one of them as your guide for that particular day. There is more than one way to be present to those in great need.

✠

ÓSCAR ROMERO (1917–1980)

Who He Was

In May 1979, Óscar Romero traveled from El Salvador to Rome where he presented the pope with seven files full of documents describing assassinations, "disappearances," and human rights abuses in El Salvador. Within a few years more than 75,000 Salvadorans were killed, one million people would flee the country, and another million were left homeless, constantly on the run from the army. Ten months later, Archbishop Romero himself was shot dead with a high-powered rifle as he celebrated Mass in the chapel of the hospital where he lived.

That Romero became an advocate for the poor was a great surprise. He was a quiet man, pious, opposed to changes in the Church and not expected to criticize the army, other bishops, or the wealthy landowners and politicians. In fact, it was expected he would reign in the priests who were speaking out for the poor. Indeed, he had consistently protected the status quo and squelched pastoral projects that he felt were too liberal.

Romero's conversion happened gradually as he became aware of the suffering of the poor. When he began to speak out forcefully and received assassination threats, he insisted on driving himself rather than endanger the life of a driver. A turning point for Romero was when Rutilio Grande, a Jesuit, was ambushed and killed along with two parishioners. Father

Rutilio had spoken out against the inhumane treatment of workers and had defended the peasant's rights to organize farm cooperatives. He said that the dogs of the big landowners ate better food than the children whose fathers worked the landowners' fields. When Archbishop Romero went to where Father Rutilio's body was taken, he knelt, held the priest's bloody corpse in his arms, and wept.

Romero preached to the army: "Brothers, you are from the same people; you kill your fellow peasant. No soldier is obliged to obey an order that is contrary to the will of God." He was assassinated on March 24, 1980. Today advocates for the poor honor him in many countries, including the United States, with shrines, memorials, and schools named after him.

His Life Speaks to Me

Óscar Romero was a convert, not to Catholicism but to the opposite viewpoint from what he held for decades. His heart was softened and his mind opened by experience, by the stories of people, and by paying attention to the Gospel rather than those in power. He paid a dear price. His fellow bishops and the wealthy families criticized him. He paid the ultimate price, his life, for following his newly discovered gospel path.

Following His Example

At a time when our Church and our nation suffer from factions that disagree sometimes loudly and strongly, we can learn a lot from Óscar Romero. We can listen and be open to those with whom we disagree. We can hold the gospel message as the final test of what we believe and how we live.

▢

PEDRO ARRUPE (1907–1991)

Who He Was

Spain, Belgium, the United States, Japan, and Italy were just a few of the places Pedro Arrupe called "home" in the course of his lifetime of eighty-four years. The reason for these travels from his original home in Bilbao, Spain, was his life as a Jesuit. Pedro became acquainted with the Jesuits while a medical student in Spain and he soon joined the order. At that time, Spain was in the midst of a civil war and the Jesuits sent him and other young men to Belgium and Holland for safety during their studies. The Jesuits were expelled from Spain and some who refused to leave were martyred. Pedro Arrupe was ordained in Belgium and sent to Jesuit theology schools in the United States, first in Kansas and then in Cleveland, where he worked with immigrants from Latin America.

A dramatic chapter in his life is his years in Japan, where he was accused of spying and spent time as a prisoner of war. Within a few years, as Jesuit Superior outside of Hiroshima, he found himself using his medical background to organize the novitiate as a place for assisting hundreds of casualties resulting from the bombing of Hiroshima at the end of World War II.

His next challenge was as Superior General of the Jesuits. For eighteen years, during the historic time following the Vatican Council, he traveled the world as their leader. Arrupe was concerned with the process of theological reflection and of evangelization through addressing human reality and human needs. A stroke paralyzed him for ten years before he died in Rome in 1991.

His Life Speaks to Me

Although Pedro Arrupe led an extraordinary life, his concerns were always very human. He was deeply concerned with human suffering in our world and the injustices that cause it. His passion for the health and well-being of those around him may have started him on the path of medicine but obviously permeated his ministry wherever he was sent. It surely was the case with the immigrants in Ohio and extraordinarily with the atomic bomb victims in Japan. Then there was his concern for his brother Jesuits as their leader for so many crucial years. He preached and lived what he called an "evangelical theology," which addressed problems of today's world such as violence and freedom by bringing human sciences and theology into conversation in order to discern what our Christian response to violence and other evils should be.

Following His Example

Pedro Arrupe went wherever he was sent, and wherever that took him he gravitated to those to whom life seemed less than fair, even cruel. None of us has to go far away to discover human suffering. As Christians, like Pedro, we cannot close our eyes and do nothing. Whether it is the simple gesture of holding someone's hand, or taking meals to the homeless, or helping our parish to respond as a community to suffering around us, there are many opportunities. Like him, we can use our prayer, our knowledge, and the experience and expertise of others to craft our own way of evangelizing by responding to basic human needs.

❧

PIERRE TEILHARD DE CHARDIN (1881–1955)

Who He Was

Pierre Teilhard de Chardin was a scientist. As a geologist and a paleontologist, he studied and worked on four continents. During World War I, he carried the stretchers of the battle wounded for his homeland, France. Pierre was also a mystic whose prayer and insights were captured in profound essays and books as a Jesuit priest. Due to concerns about his theological views, he found himself forbidden by Church officials on numerous occasions to speak publicly or to publish his writings.

However, since his death in 1955, not only have more than twenty volumes of his writings been published, but they are acclaimed by the Church and have been helpful to the spirituality of so many people. His work as a scientist is appreciated worldwide. In the years since 1955, his religious order as well as his Church reversed themselves and proudly claimed him. On the one hundredth anniversary of his death, Pope John Paul II praised him for precisely what he was criticized for during his life—helping Christians comfortably accept science, using it and relating it to faith, helping Catholics see that evolution can be embraced, and furthermore, that ours is not a religion of individuals but of an entire people who should be working to build up the earth.

His Life Speaks to Me

From the time he was a young man in France, Pierre knew he had a special calling and generously and unselfishly followed it. He could have no idea the suffering and deprivation his brilliance in science and his mystical insights would cause him. Although there were repeated times when he was denied the ability to use his gifts publicly, he persevered with incredible humility through his entire lifetime of rejection. Pierre Teilhard de Chardin was exiled to China for twenty years by his superiors and later exiled to New York, where he died of a heart attack on the day he always wished for his death—Easter, the feast of the Resurrection.

Following His Example

In the course of a lifetime, many people say that one of the hardest things to accept is to be misunderstood. Can we even imagine what it was like for Pierre, a deeply spiritual mystic and a brilliant scientist, to have his ideas so misunderstood that he was exiled and kept from sharing them during his lifetime? Perhaps not, but we can look around at the people near us who are misunderstood or not accepted for much less serious reasons, and we can open our minds and hearts to them. We can decide not to keep ourselves ignorant of other religions and other points of view, not to be afraid or judgmental of learning, and even to challenge our own prejudices.

From his example, we can take heart if we seem to pray and listen to the Spirit in a way that others may find unconventional or strange. We can expand our understanding of the Catholic faith from being a "Jesus and me" spirituality to one that is inclusive and concerned for the entire Body of Christ. We can celebrate the Eucharist as community prayer and work in social outreach to improve the entire community, not just ourselves.

✦

PIERRE TOUSSAINT (1766–1853)

Who He Was

Pierre Toussaint was born a slave child in 1766 in Haiti. A Frenchman, Jean Berard, owned the family. Pierre's family were house slaves as opposed to field slaves. They were treated well and baptized with the Berard family. As a young boy, Pierre was taught to read and could even use the family library when he wanted to. At about the age of ten, the Berards moved to New York City, bringing Pierre and his sister Rosalie with them.

Pierre's owner apprenticed him to a hairdresser so that he could learn a trade. Eventually his outstanding skill earned him customers among the elite of New York, including the wife of Alexander Hamilton. Pierre became a trusted confidant to them as well. He listened to their serious difficulties and advised them to do as he himself did, pray over their problems and trust in God, promising that he would pray for them also.

After Jean Berard died, Pierre refused his widow's offer of freedom, as he knew she needed him to continue to support the family with his hairdresser's income. He continued to go to early Mass, return home to do the work in the household, and then take care of his appointments. It was only when Mrs. Berard remarried that he accepted her offer of freedom. Now he was able to marry the Haitian woman he loved, Juliette Noel. Over the years they took into their home many orphans and destitute people, especially slaves and black children. Their home became an employment agency, a credit union, and a place of refuge for many. Toussaint's successful business enabled him and his wife to be generous benefactors for churches, religious communities, and schools.

His Life Speaks to Me

Over the many years that Pierre Toussaint lived in New York, two things never changed. He always experienced prejudice and he always maintained a remarkable internal peace. Insults were common for both blacks and Catholics then, and he even experienced discrimination in the Church. He was once turned away from a church door by an usher because of his race. Ironically this was a church he himself had helped build. However, Pierre knew that nothing and no one could take away his dignity as a person because God gave that to him.

Following His Example

At sometime in our life almost everyone experiences some form of prejudice. Like Pierre, it may be because of our race, or it may be that we are too young, too old, or the wrong sex, or it may be because of our religion. We can learn from him not to let other's prejudging affect how we act, even toward them. Remembering how Pierre handled such incidents can give us courage and grace. From him we can also learn to examine our own attitudes toward people from whom we are different. How would Pierre act? How would Jesus act? We also have in him a wonderful model of taking our problems to God in prayer as he did and as he advised his many confidants to do. Then we listen with an open heart and act on what we hear inside ourselves as God's voice.

✠

ROSE HAWTHORNE LATHROP (1851–1926)

Who She Was

"Rosebud," as her father, Nathaniel Hawthorne, the writer called her, lived a life of privilege, heartbreak, and courage. She was born into a literary family and spent her early years among the cultural elite of New York's society. However, both of Rose's parents died when she was a young teenager. She suffered the death of her only child when he was just four years old. Later she ended her marriage to an alcoholic husband. Alone in New York City, Rose discovered that her friend, Emma Lazarus, whose inscription is on the Statue of Liberty, had cancer. At that time, cancer was an especially dreaded disease. Believed to be contagious, it was incurable and fiercely painful with little treatment available. While Emma received good care, Rose learned that poor people with cancer were sent to the grim Blackwell's Island, New York City's last resort for the penniless.

At the age of forty-four, Rose felt she had finally discovered what she was supposed to do with the rest of her life. She took a nursing course and courageously moved to a poor section of the city, where she went from door to door giving care to the sick. Soon her apartment became a hospice for cancer sufferers. The first person she took in was a seven-year-old boy. She changed patients' dressings, bathed them and fed them, became their friend and their protector. Eventually her wealthy friend, Alice Huber, joined her and together they eventually founded the Hawthorne Dominican Sisters. Rose and Alice became known as Sister Alphonsa and Sister Mary Rose and opened a second home for the patients in Hawthorne, New York.

Today this community of religious sisters still provides a home and care for incurable cancer patients who cannot afford care elsewhere. All care is free. No payments are accepted either from patients or their families, or from Medicare, Medicaid, or private insurance.

Her Life Speaks to Me

Out of a life of privilege, heartbreak, and courage, Rose Hawthorne entered each chapter of her life with hope and a desire to do the right thing. Her extraordinary life is not one whose exact footsteps we follow, but it is an example to meditate on and emulate in our own way. Each time a door closed for her, she found a way to "reinvent" herself and find a purpose for her life.

Following Her Example

Rose Hawthorne's life can teach us that when tragedy or hardship comes our way, we should take time to grieve, then assess the situation and move forward. So often, we can discover the courage and purpose we never knew we had because we, like Rose Hawthorne, are really never alone. Wherever we may find ourselves presently in our lives, we can take some time to care for the sick. This may be done by a personal visit, writing a note, sending a card, or spending time in prayer. Like Rose, we will receive more than we ever give.

✦

ROSE PHILIPPINE DUCHESNE (1769–1852)

Who She Was

Imagine spending more than four months on the Atlantic Ocean and Mississippi River in the early nineteenth century in the less than luxurious vessels of the day. This was not a vacation cruise but what Rose Philippine Duchesne did in order to fulfill her lifelong dream of being a missionary to America.

At baptism, Rose Philippine received the names of Rose of Lima and Philip, the apostle. She was born and raised in a wealthy French family. When she was a young woman, she joined the cloistered convent of the Visitation Sisters against her parents' wishes. This defiant action was only one sign of the strong determination that would serve her well in the challenging paths that lay ahead. During the French Revolution, the religious orders were suppressed and when her convent disbanded, she returned home, devoting herself to nursing prisoners. After the French Revolution, she and a few of the nuns tried to return to their convent, but the buildings were in hopeless disrepair and it was not to be.

However, Rose was determined to stay on the path she had chosen and in 1804, she learned of a new congregation, the Society of the Sacred Heart of Jesus, and joined them. Her dream was to go to the new world in America as a missionary. After twelve years, her dream was realized and she set off across the Atlantic to New Orleans and up the Mississippi River to St. Louis. There, in St. Charles, Missouri, she lived in a log cabin with all the challenges of frontier life and learned English. She eventually founded schools for Native Americans and for young women. Again, she wanted to push the boundaries and go farther west. At the age of seventy-two, she moved to Sugar Creek in what is now Kansas to work with the Jesuits. She was in frail health and the Native Americans called her "Woman Who Prays Always." Rose Philippine Duchesne returned to St. Charles for her last decade of life and she died there in 1852.

Her Life Speaks to Me

We can only imagine the hardship of life for these French nuns on the frontier in St. Charles, with the cold weather, lack of food, and their difficulty with the English language. None of this overcame the determination of Rose and her companions. She was obviously willing to endure any hardship to live out the dream, the vision that called to her in her heart. She was willing to sacrifice herself so that young women would have an opportunity to be educated and so that the Native Americans would have the chance to hear the Gospel.

Following Her Example

Life involves sacrifices of some kind: giving up sleep for young children, foregoing comforts for their education, leaving a job to care for elderly parents in need, giving up time to volunteer for a worthy cause. Rose shows us how to stay focused no matter what obstacles try to keep us from doing the right thing. Her spirit of generosity without complaint can remind us to reach for the same. We should encourage and thank those whom we see making sacrifices while we look for what we ourselves can do.

⚊

SOLANUS CASEY (1870–1957)

Who He Was

Solanus Casey loved baseball, especially the Detroit Tigers. He also enjoyed hot dogs smothered in onions and playing his violin, which his friends agreed he played rather poorly. When his fellow Capuchin monks saw him coming with violin in hand, they would quickly find something they had to do. Solanus would just take his violin to the chapel and play it in front of the Blessed Sacrament. Not being offended was typical of this down-to-earth man. In fact, he had no pretensions about anything else he did either.

Solanus, the name of a Spanish missionary who worked with the poor, was the name Bernard Francis Casey took when he joined the Capuchin Order at the age of twenty-one. He was from a large family of Irish immigrant farmers in Wisconsin, and Bernard had a number of jobs before he entered religious life. He worked as a prison guard, a hospital orderly, and as a logger. As a Capuchin, he was given the simplest of jobs such as greeting visitors and taking care of sacristy duties. Although he was ordained as a priest, the community did not allow him to preach or hear confessions because he had done poorly as a theology student.

However, during his time in Detroit, in New York, and later again in Detroit, he had an enormous effect on the many people whose lives he touched. Solanus began to hold services for the sick and before long, two hundred people came each day to receive his blessing. Eventually it became typical for one hundred people a day to come to see him and to bring their troubles to him. He would listen patiently to each person's problems, giving comfort and advice. Many people claimed he had cured them or the person they had prayed about with him. It was during the Depression that he began handing out food from his office and that was the start of the Capuchin Soup Kitchen in Detroit. Solanus lived to be eighty-seven years old.

His Life Speaks to Me

When people tried to give him credit for healings or cures they attributed to him, Solanus would dismiss any notion that it was because of him. His most common words were, "Thanks be to God." He lived without pretensions, with an open heart and mind, and certainly with "open ears" to hear the needs of the people who came and sat with him.

Following His Example

We only have one life to live and sometimes people want to do great things with this one life. Solanus can show us that the goal can be to realize what you do *is* great if you use the gifts God gave you and if you live with the right spirit of generosity and thankfulness in your heart. His humility, his humor, and his ability to stay down-to-earth are wonderful qualities we can emulate in our own way, in our own life. Like Solanus, we can begin and end each day with the grateful prayer, "Thanks be to God."

❧

TERESA OF AVILA (1515–1582)

Who She Was

This well-known Spanish woman is one of the thirty-three people named "Doctors" by the Church, with only three of them being women. This designation puts them on a plane with those whose writings and preaching is useful for people throughout the ages. They are considered especially brilliant in their theological teachings. Though not infallible, they are proposed as guides and each is held by the Church to have contributed in great significance to our understanding of Christian teaching. Indeed Teresa fits all the qualifications. Her writings, *The Way of Perfection* and *The Interior Castle*, both clearly show her great mind as well as her remarkable spiritual experiences and insights.

In sixteenth-century Carmelite convents in Spain, the women were often from wealthy Spanish families and spent much of their time in the convent parlor entertaining and visiting with their friends. Teresa set out to change this by forming the Discalced Carmelites, who lived very simply, stayed behind cloister doors, ate a vegetarian diet, and grew their own food. Their prayer life was strict and intense. Before her death, Teresa had founded sixteen such convents. She wrote books only because she was told by her religious superior to write about her own prayer life in order to help some of the other nuns who were having difficulty praying. Although Teresa wrote reluctantly, as a result of them, generations of people have been helped and inspired by her works, which are considered classics.

Her Life Speaks to Me

Though an extraordinary mystic, Teresa was able to teach and guide ordinary people in their spiritual life. She believed firmly in the presence of God in every person and would often say that we do not need wings to find God but only need to look inside of ourselves. Her most famous saying has comforted and given strength to so many people: "Let nothing trouble you, let nothing make you afraid. All things pass away. Only God never changes. Patience. God alone is enough."

Following Her Example

Life is about the basics. Teresa shows us the importance of prayer. Her style of prayer may seem extraordinary, but it was her own conversation with God and openness to whatever happened if she took the time to be just in the presence of God. We can do that too, and we will be changed in ways we do not even know. Teresa believed so strongly in God's presence in human beings. Each time we are with another person, we can remind ourselves that God dwells in him or her. Imagine how this can shape our ordinary relationships. When we are troubled, her wonderful quote can give us courage and comfort knowing that this, too, will pass, and God is with us no matter what.

❖

THEA BOWMAN (1937–1990)

Who She Was

A young black girl was sent to a Catholic school in rural Mississippi. Who could imagine the consequences of that decision both for her and for many, many people in her future? At the age of ten, Thea asked her parents to let her be baptized a Catholic. This step eventually led her to enter the convent of the Franciscan Sisters of Perpetual Adoration. This religious community appreciated her wonderful mind. She thrived as a student, eventually earning her doctorate in English from The Catholic University of America. Thea's education served her well as a teacher in elementary school, high school, and university.

The name Thea means "of God" and though her life was brief, she challenged many people, from children to bishops, to be "of God" themselves. Sister Thea was passionate about her black heritage and became a tireless advocate for appreciating the gift of the African American culture to the Catholic Church in the United States. She brought song, dance, and preaching to countless audiences as she traveled not only in her own country but throughout the world as a much-sought-after speaker at Catholic conferences. No one who "experienced" Thea forgot her. She would preach dramatically, stop, and sing in a rich, full voice with the audience clapping and singing along. She roused an assembled group of bishops to their feet singing "We Shall Overcome" at the end of her presentation to them.

This granddaughter of a slave brought her ministry of joy and challenge far beyond her Mississippi roots. When Thea was diagnosed with cancer, she said that her prayer became, "Lord, let me live until I die." Thea did live fully to the last minute of her life. Some would say she was at her peak when she died of cancer, still singing and challenging audiences from her wheelchair to the end.

Her Life Speaks to Me

Thea appreciated how gifted she was and throughout her brief life, she used her intelligence, her ideas, her voice, and her very presence for God to challenge all those she came in contact with. She expected much from herself and of everyone she met. She spoke to all Catholics when she said that even though women were not allowed to preach in her church, they and every single Christian should preach everywhere else. "Preach by word, by love, by faith, by witness," she would say.

Following Her Example

Do not shortchange any day. Do not shortchange yourself by hiding your talents. Thea's talents were easily recognized by herself, those who guided her religious life, and those who were touched by her life. Sometimes we need to work hard to name and appreciate the tools that God has placed within us to use during our own life. Sometimes an honest friend and confidant is needed to affirm or name for us what we may not see in ourselves. Then it is a matter between you and God and your life circumstances to do as Thea prayed, "Lord, let me live until I die!" and not waste what God has put there.

⬩

ANNE-THÉRÈSE GUÉRIN (1798–1856)

Who She Was

In a life shorter than six decades Anne-Thérèse Guérin, or Mother Théodore as she later became known, lived a life that she, with the feelings of unworthiness she carried, must have been more than surprised at. She started a college for women, St. Mary of the Woods in Indiana, and lived through harsh Midwestern winters in a log cabin with the other women in her religious order. She also experienced great prejudice against Catholics by the people in the area. In addition, their entire harvest was destroyed by fire, leaving the sisters not only hungry, but also destitute in a foreign land. They had previously endured a terrifying journey from France by steamboat, railroad, canal boat, and stagecoach to reach their destination. To their astonishment when they arrived, they discovered they were not in a town, but in a log cabin in the midst of the woods of Indiana. The ten women had been sent by their religious order to assist Father Beteux, who needed the nuns to begin schools in that mission territory.

This was not the life Anne-Thérèse had imagined at all. She was a young woman educated at home in France by her mother, Isabelle, whose lessons focused on scripture and religion. Her father, serving in Napoleon's navy, was away from home sometimes for years. When Anne-Thérèse was fifteen, she took over the responsibility of the family when bandits murdered her father on his way home to visit. It was not until she was twenty-five that she finally entered the convent, which had been a goal of hers since childhood. By the time of her death, Mother Théodore had opened schools throughout Indiana. She is buried at St. Mary of the Woods, Indiana, in the church of the Immaculate Conception.

Her Life Speaks to Me

Mother Théodore had her life planned out. She would join the convent as soon as she was old enough. However, when life gave her surprises, such as her father's untimely death or the primitive existence during the early years in Indiana, she persevered. She took care of her family as long as she was needed. During hard times, she sustained herself with a rich prayer life and the community friendships she developed. Her sense of responsibility served her well and helped her accomplish many things during her life.

Following Her Example

For those who have their lives planned out, Mother Théodore can teach how to accept surprises, small or dramatic, and give the new path your best efforts. For those who do not have a plan for the future, her example is equally true. For all people, she shows the importance of a spirituality of trust and hope.

✦

THÉRÈSE OF LISIEUX (1873–1897)

Who She Was

For a woman who died at the age of twenty-four, Thérèse has had a great influence on a remarkable number of people. Thérèse believed that the spiritual life could and should be practical and simple; it was for everyone, not just for religious and certainly not just for extraordinarily holy men and women. Although she was a cloistered Carmelite nun, Thérèse has become a model for many laypeople to imitate. She disagreed with the traditional medieval path of self-mortification and visionary experiences and followed a more straightforward spiritual path herself. Therese chose to put the liturgy and reading of the Scriptures at the center of her spiritual life, along the lines of the spiritual renewal of the Second Vatican.

Life in the convent was made especially difficult for her due to her poor health and because the community was very rigid and divided into factions as a result of the temperament of the superior. Thérèse was a prayerful person but in her own way. She had hoped to volunteer to go to the missions but was unable to because of her health. She chose to write letters of encouragement to those who were serving there, especially two particular missionaries whom she adopted spiritually. Besides her letters, Thérèse also wrote poetry and a short autobiography, *The Story of a Soul*. She died of tuberculosis.

Her Life Speaks to Me

Her steadfastness in prayer and confidence in God when life's path did not go where she had hoped is a reminder to all who want to imitate Thérèse. Life in the convent was not what she had hoped and her dream of going to the missions was unfulfilled. However, she prayed and had confidence that she could do God's will where she was. Her reading and study of the Scriptures sustained her while the liturgy itself that was at the heart of her life.

Following Her Example

Some people know where they are going in life. They have a very clear idea of what they should do with this one life that they have been given. Sometimes their life turns out that way and sometimes it does not. Others do not dream or see ahead but take life as it comes. Both of these types of people can use Thérèse's prayerful confidence in God in making the most of each day living on this earth. While we pray in many ways, we learn an important lesson from Thérèse's priority to the Sacred Liturgy that was the center of her life. Likewise, studying and reading the Scriptures that may be seen as our Church family history tell us the story of how to be the person Christ wants us to be by following the directives He gives us in his preaching and his example.

✦

THOMAS MERTON (1915–1968)

Who He Was

Thomas Merton was an English teacher. His mother, who was from Ohio, died when he was six years old. His father, a painter, decided to take Thomas and his brother to live in France and later in England. However, his father died when Thomas was a teenager. Though without religious upbringing, as a young adult Merton became interested in Christianity. He studied the faith and was baptized a Catholic.

Thomas taught English at St. Bonaventure's College in upstate New York for a few years before moving to Harlem to work with the poor. Still an aspiring novelist, he was drawn to the contemplative life. After his second visit to Gethsemane Abbey in Kentucky, he tore up the two novels he was writing and gave his clothes and everything he owned to the poor. At twenty-six years of age, Merton traded the classroom for the monastery and writing novels for spiritual writing. Eventually he became one of the great spiritual writers of the twentieth century, with his *Seven Storey Mountain* autobiography becoming a classic. Thomas lived for twenty-six years as a cloistered monk. Ironically, Thomas Merton died in the Far East at a Buddhist conference when a faulty electric fan accidentally electrocuted him.

His Life Speaks to Me

Merton was an intellectual and a mystic, which may put him in a totally different category than the rest of us. However, he went through life—whether visiting an art museum in Manhattan or walking in the forest in Kentucky —with his eyes and ears open to all that was around him. Perhaps this was his secret to a rich spiritual life. Thomas did not allow himself to be separated from God's creation nor from people, lest he be separated from what brought him closer to God. Thomas not only kept his eyes and ears opened, but he intentionally *used* them as windows to allow the goodness of God into his consciousness.

Following His Example

We may not spend our lives in a monastery, but we do spend it in God's own magnificent world. Not all of what we see and hear is beautiful. However, we are called to be attentive to daily living so that we do not miss the gifts of God that are beautiful. Notice the smile on the face of the person we pass on the street or in the hall. Pay attention so that we see the humor in the ordinary events of the day and smile at them. Recognize the many signs of goodness in the people in our lives. Say a silent thank you to God in our prayer when we do have these experiences. Living in the presence of God in this way makes us mystics in our own ordinary life.

✦

THOMAS MORE (1478–1535)

Who He Was

St. Thomas More is the most famous victim of King Henry VIII's persecution of Catholics who refused to accept the king as the head of the Church. After spending fifteen months in prison, Thomas More was beheaded for this stance, as were many other people. This was a man who was both quite ordinary and quite exceptional in all parts of his life.

Thomas More had a strong belief in the importance of ordinary family life. When his wife died, leaving him to raise four children, he chose to marry a widow who would be a good mother to them. The family prayed together and often read the Scriptures at the dinner table. Their family life was lively, filled with many visitors coming and going, often travelers or people in high positions. Although he was one of the most respected men of his time as both a lawyer and judge, Thomas had little ambition for worldly success. Nevertheless even the king, before their ultimate disagreement, chose him repeatedly for leadership positions. Thomas was popular as a judge, especially among the poor, because he did not favor the rich and was fair and quick in his judgments. Thomas More is the patron of lawyers, judges, and those in public office.

His Life Speaks to Me

Thomas More took education seriously, both his own and for his children. He was exceptional in his day for seeing that his daughters were well educated. Although involved in serious matters as a lawyer and judge, he was known for his sense of humor. Even as Thomas was being beheaded, he moved his beard from the block because, he said, it had not offended the king. His motto to the end was, "I die the king's good servant, but God's first." Over the years, his dedication to prayer caused him to set aside Friday as a special day of prayer each week.

Following His Example

We can learn a lot about the sacred task of raising a child from this father. Although he was often indirectly involved, Thomas ensured that the values of a family life rich with loving care, education, and prayer were part of his children's experience. These priorities and values are timeless and important for us at any age in our own life. Surrounding ourselves with people who care for us and for whom we care gives a strong foundation for staying on course in our life. Seeing that we structure prayer time in a busy life is another value of his worth emulating. Like both Thomas and his children, the importance of ongoing education helps us use all the gifts God placed in us. The combination of these priorities will help us stay true to our values regardless of how they are challenged.

◀◆▶

VINCENT DE PAUL (1580–1660)

Who He Was

Ironically, this poor farm boy who spent his early years trying to escape the life into which he was born became the man "for God and for the poor," as he described himself later in life. His parents thought that if Vincent became a priest it would help him out of their terrible poverty, which it did. As a priest, Vincent rose to the highest levels of French society, becoming chaplain to Queen Margaret of Valois. This position brought him the financial support of many benefactors and he lived a good life.

When Vincent was middle aged and visiting the owners of an estate, he was asked to hear the confession of a dying peasant who lived on the grounds. This simple but profound event reminded Vincent of the seriousness of his vocation as a priest. He determined to change directions and dedicated himself to the service of the poor. He did this in a dramatic and long-lasting way. The Vincentians, the order of priests he founded, worked in the countryside in the spiritual formation of the poor, going from village to village to preach. The education of secular clergy was at a low point so the Vincentians began teaching in seminaries. Vincent's wealthy friends helped finance his many charitable endeavors. Louise de Marillac, one of these friends, eventually founded the Daughters of Charity, which was also devoted to the poor and the sick. Vincent told these nuns,

"When you leave your prayer to care for a sick person, you leave God for God. To care for a sick person is to pray."

In time, Vincent's work became so widespread and effective that wealthy people competed to fund his projects. These projects included hospitals, orphanages, homes for mentally disabled, and ministries to prisoners and slaves. He is the patron saint of charitable societies and works.

His Life Speaks to Me

Vincent was a bright and ambitious man. He was clear about his goal in life—to get out of the poor class in his society. Vincent did not just set his goals once and for all. When he reexamined what he was doing, he had the courage to go in a very different direction. He understood the importance of ongoing formation in faith. Though parts of his life are unclear, it seems he took time in Rome for study, and then committed himself to educating all people in the Church, from the poor villagers to the seminarians.

Following His Example

Vincent was a practical man whose life offers many aspects and qualities to imitate. Among them are his commitment to ongoing faith formation for laity, turning away from things that take us away from a godly life, and the basic process of continuing to examine our conscience about the priorities in life. Vincent was doing good things while he was living the good life, but when he stopped to look at it, he saw that he could do better. Perhaps we can do the same as well.

The Catholic Prayer Bible (NRSV): *Lectio Divina* Edition

An ideal Bible for anyone who desires to reflect on the individual stories and chapters of just one, or even all, of the biblical books, while being led to prayer though meditation on that biblical passage.

978-0-8091-0587-8 1968 pp. $39.95 Hardcover

978-0-8091-4663-5 1968 pp. $29.95 Paperback

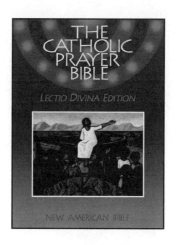

Becoming Who You Are: Insights on the True Self from Thomas Merton and Other Saints

James Martin, SJ
HiddenSpring Books

By meditating on personal examples from the author's life, as well as reflecting on the inspirational life and writings of Thomas Merton, stories from the Gospels, as well as the lives of other holy men and women (among them, Henri Nouwen, Thérèse of Lisieux and Pope John XXIII) the reader will see how becoming who you are, and becoming the person that God created, is a simple path to happiness, peace of mind and even sanctity.

1-58768-036-X 112 pp. $10.00 Paperback